THE **TRUE YOU**

Enjoy!
Emma

Praise for

THE TRUE YOU

"Mastering the patterns and habits of our thought processes is key to success in life and business. *The True You* will give you the insights and tools you will need to develop strong relationships, which are key to enjoying your life. It will help you free yourself from habits that are not serving you, and build new ones."

—**Paul David Walker**, adviser to CEOs and founder of Genius Stone Partners, author of *Invent Your Future: Starting With Your Calling, Unleashing Genius: Leading Yourself, Teams and Corporations* and three other books.

"Gentle, yet powerful beyond measure, Emma helps you understand who you think you are and why, then takes you on a journey to uncover who you really are. Lifting your mind to a vantage point where you can see your entire life and the people in it with fresh eyes, dissolving any thinking that holds you back from living the life you desire and the one you came here to live. *The True You* is a classic—it will inspire you to see your world in a very different way."

—**Elaine Kennedy McIvor**, author of *The CheerLeaders & Vampires in Your Life*

"This is the sort of book you will treasure and keep coming back to. It is filled with powerful ideas and techniques that remove stress and make your life easier and more joyful."

—**Clare Moore**, author of *A Buyer's Guide to Business Coaching*.

"If you want to get to know people better, especially yourself, you must read *The True You*. If you think you don't need to read this book . . . then you *definitely* need to read it! The author, Emma J. Bell, is without a doubt one of the most inspirational people I have ever met, and when you read this book you will clearly see why."

—**Wendy McQueen**, founder and CEO, Artisan Cheesecakes

"A refreshing, thought-provoking read. Emma shares her personal experiences and practical insights for individuals who truly want to develop personal relationships through growth and inspiration."

—**Nikki Donaldson**, Chief Executive, Fife Housing Association

"*The True You* is fantastic—a great development tool, guide and companion—and useful no matter at what stage of life's journey you find yourself. I would recommend this book to anyone and everyone."

—**Joyce White**, Chief Executive, West Dunbartonshire Council

"*The True You* is the perfect companion for everyone who wants to truly understand themselves and pursue their real purpose in life. It is filled with meaningful explanations as to why we think the way we do, and fascinating insights into deep-rooted thinking patterns. *The True You* helps us advance from old, unproductive thoughts to new, positive feelings and actions, and guides us toward genuine meaning in our lives. Carry it with you and build the most important relationship you'll ever have: the relationship with yourself and your leader within— the true you."

—**Karen Anderson**, Director, Anderson Business Development

"*The True You* is engaging, inspiring and completely draws you in wanting more—and wanting to change! Emma has the remarkable ability to take the theory and make it practical which in turn makes business and personal challenges entirely achievable. She is truly an inspiring individual."

—**Joanne Brooks**, HR Director

"Reading this book provides a wonderful insight into living the best life you can—it is like having a calm, supportive, and friendly hand on your shoulder, guiding you to being the best you can."

—**Jacqui Jones**, HR Director

"Emma has captured the essence of why it is so important to understand the value of relationships in both personal and business settings. This book will nudge you toward a clearer understanding of how your relationship with yourself can improve every interaction with others. *The True You* is a true companion in this journey of improvement."

—**Anne Marie Forsyth**, Chief Executive, CCA

Praise for
EMMA J. BELL

"Emma has a steely determination to seek out the management challenges many would shy away from, but she does so with a perceptive understanding of each individual's strengths and potential to lead. Her style is warm, calm and engaging but her purpose is resolute. Her approach is founded on the maxim that 'behaviors breed behaviors'—that our values and behaviors as leaders must exemplify the change we wish to see in our people. Emma's influence on our leadership development was so well received it has become the bedrock of a new strategy for the whole firm. With Emma's leadership, we are now focused on stronger relationships within our workplace, which we know will have a positive impact on our work and our clients. In the great babble of leadership manuals, Emma's is an intelligent voice worth listening to."

—**Gareth Magee**, Partner, Scott Moncrieff, LLP

"Emma is a uniquely talented individual who has the ability to offer imaginative and effective solutions to difficult behavioral and relationship situations. This is always offered in a supportive and encouraging way focusing on nurturing the talent of each individual to enable them to succeed and fulfill their full potential."

—**Elizabeth Dickson**, HR Specialist

"I first met Emma during the tender process to support our firm's leadership development program. I selected Emma due to her credible background of working with professional service firms and, more importantly, her ability to establish the requirements of the program at our initial meeting. Emma helped me to shape my thinking into a practical but inspiring program, and while working with Emma, I felt extremely motivated and excited about the results of the program.

Emma's initial meetings with partners, directors and managers were a fantastic success; she generated an environment where senior partners shared key business problems, and Emma's incredible coaching style identified goals to be achieved by both the business and individuals. Emma's credible background and amazing coaching style creates fantastic opportunities for people to develop themselves. Personally, Emma has helped me to tackle some very challenging situations and behaviors. She achieves this in an incredibly positive way with a no-nonsense practical approach."

—**Joanne Brooks**, HR Director

"Emma's input is always highly practical and focused on supporting leaders to get the most out of themselves and others. Emma is extremely knowledgeable and perceptive in her interactions with the audience, and leaves individuals feeling inspired and empowered to make changes to their habits and interactions with others in order to fulfill personal potential and develop effective relationships."

—**Nicola Dudley**, Deputy Director,
Scottish Council of Independent Schools

"Emma discovers and resolves the issues and barriers which might be severely limiting business and personal performance and yet can be too difficult for a board or an organization to acknowledge. She does this sensitively and incisively. Working with Emma improved my understanding of organizational behavior and conflict resolution and made a significant contribution to my personal development, and thus my career."

—**Donald Forsyth**, Partner, Ernst and Young, LLP

"I and my colleagues on the senior staff team at Link engaged Emma to get us onto the leadership development journey some four years ago, and we have since taken advantage of—and benefited greatly from—embedding what we learned throughout the Link Group of social enterprise companies. And we have recently reengaged her to review how we've done.

'Leadership' is a complicated and oft-misunderstood concept—but Emma 'gets it!' And by the time you've been through the process, you've 'got it' too.

That's not to say that it's painless. We all have the confidence in our views that 'goes with the job,' but Emma quietly and firmly sets about disturbing our comfort zones—and sends us away at the end of each session with a sore head. But in the morning, you wake up refreshed, and behaving and acting better.

In short, she's brilliant; and working with her is an enlightening and rewarding experience."

—**Craig Sanderson**, Chief Executive, Link Group Ltd.

"I have had the pleasure of working closely with Emma for five years now. During that time, Emma has made a significant contribution to the training and development programs at the firm, taking the lead on creating, developing and running leadership development programs for our partner and associate groups. Feedback on the sessions is consistently positive, and I can honestly say that her work has helped us to shape how we conduct ourselves in the business. Over this period, Emma has also operated as a coach for a number of people. Again, the feedback is always positive, and there are real tangible examples of how Emma has made a difference. Emma's approach to leadership training and coaching is innovative and creative, and more importantly, she has been able to influence change, truly getting the best out of people."

—**Kirstie MacLennan**, HR Director

"Emma played an instrumental role in helping us to reorder our priorities and to formulate practical steps toward changing our behaviors and actions. Her coaching and facilitation were critical to the success of our leadership development program; and her common sense insights, in relation to organizational culture and individual self-improvement, meant that even the most reluctant participants feel they have benefited greatly."

—**Paul Renz**, Partner, Scott Moncrieff, LLP

THE
TRUE YOU

Discover Your Own Way to Success and Happiness
by Uncovering Your Authentic Self and Building
Remarkable Relationships With Others

EMMA J. BELL

New York

THE **TRUE YOU**

Discover Your Own Way to Success and Happiness by Uncovering Your
Authentic Self and Building Remarkable Relationships With Others

© 2016 **EMMA J. BELL**.

Published in New York, New York, by Morgan James Publishing. Morgan James and The
Entrepreneurial Publisher are trademarks of Morgan James, LLC.
www.MorganJamesPublishing.com

The Morgan James Speakers Group can bring authors to your live event. For more information or
to book an event visit The Morgan James Speakers Group at
www.TheMorganJamesSpeakersGroup.com.

Shelfie

A **free** eBook edition is available
with the purchase of this print book.

CLEARLY PRINT YOUR NAME ABOVE IN UPPER CASE

Instructions to claim your free eBook edition:
1. Download the Shelfie app for Android or iOS
2. Write your name in **UPPER CASE** above
3. Use the Shelfie app to submit a photo
4. Download your eBook to any device

ISBN 978-1-63047-761-5 paperback
ISBN 978-1-63047-763-9 eBook
ISBN 978-1-63047-764-6 audio
ISBN 978-1-63047-762-2 hardcover
Library of Congress Control Number:
2015914562

Cover Design by:
Chris Treccani
www.3dogdesign.net

Interior Design by:
Bonnie Bushman
The Whole Caboodle Graphic Design

In an effort to support local communities and raise awareness and funds, Morgan James
Publishing donates a percentage of all book sales for the life of each book to Habitat for
Humanity Peninsula and Greater Williamsburg.

Get involved today, visit
www.MorganJamesBuilds.com

Habitat
for Humanity®
Peninsula and
Greater Williamsburg
Building Partner

For Graeme:

Thank you for showing me how
wonderful it feels to be loved unconditionally.

CONTENTS

FOREWORD

Like a way-too-early-bird, the phlebotomist burst into the room with a chipper, "Do you mind if I turn on the overhead light?"

From his hospital bed, my husband, Dale, groaned in his sleep, and from the recliner next to him, I pulled a thick eye-cover over my face. It kept the light out, but not the commotion that followed. One by one, and in quick succession, different medically necessary persons made their entrance like vaudeville acts vying for top billing.

First, there was the lady who came for blood. Next came the flamboyant electrocardiogram technician. After him trailed the night nurse, the charge nurse, and the staff of the nutrition-support department.

It was now shift-change time. A new nurse came in, followed by the physician's assistant, who, by the way, was worth taking my blindfold off for. He asked the unassuming woman from housekeeping to come back later. She turned around and bumped into the internal-transportation specialist just arriving to take Dale to the radiologist. And finally, like the ringmaster himself, the doctor appeared. "Can we go home?" Dale asked.

Like a crowded hospital room over which we seemingly have little control, our thoughts take on a life and momentum of their own, piling in, one on top of the other: bossing, intimidating and frankly, confusing us. After a lifetime of submission to these pseudo-authorities, how refreshing, how empowering, how liberating to learn that we don't have to acquiesce to their conflicting agendas. We have the power!

For me personally, Emma Bell's charge to take charge could not have come at a better time.

Earlier this year, my team and I attended a conference/seminar about sharing our passion and expertise with the world. In that high energy, information-packed environment, we became newly endowed prophets: visionary and fearless, ready to lead multitudes over mountains, to plant flags atop summits, to blaze trails through lands of promise.

And then we got home.

Little by little, Doubt and Fear elbowed their way into the room, cramming out Visionary and Fearless, until our mission was so hijacked, so dubious, so ridiculous by their reckoning, that despite protests from Reassurance, Reason and Logic, I was ready to abort.

That's when Emma asked me to read her book. Thank goodness.

Emma Bell and I had met and hit it off at the same seminar I just referred to—the one that ignited my flame for doing "good" by doing my best for the world. When she and I parted at the seminar's conclusion, she was full of the same vim, vigor and vision that I was, but managed somehow to sidestep a crisis of faith. Her roar never faltered. How? Why?

The answers are in this book.

Emma thinks, to this day, that I agreed to read the manuscript as a favor to her. The truth is, I agreed to read it as a favor to myself. I was all too ready to learn her secrets, to become her fellow and her follower, eager to put myself in her place, even as she put herself in mine—which, by the way, is the hallmark of an exceptional author. I was not disappointed. Her beautiful, candid confessions invited me to examine Emma "the person," while her rock-solid research, specific instruction, promising perspectives, and real examples persuaded me to study Emma "the professional." As a result, she guided me through the sometimes frightening and always thrilling quest for self-discovery and mastery; and in the end, as I hoped, I am once again atop the prophet's mountain, quite determined this time not to slip from the summit. I know now that if I do, it will be by my own hand, not anyone else's. The room in my head where such things are decided, the room so long contested and so long congested, has been cleared of all influences that are not my own.

Thank you, Emma Bell. My initial admiration of the externally confidant and charismatic woman has only exploded into veneration for the internally calm and compassionate one. The world will be so much the better, the brighter, the clearer for the way Emma has led us all into becoming leaders: chiefly in our relationship with ourselves, and consequentially, in the relationships we have with others. In addition to recommending the reading of this book to everyone, including all my family and friends, I know thousands of women will feel Emma's message coming through me. Their marriages will be blessed because their hearts will be enlarged because their heads will be their own. I wish you all, every reader and every follower, a grand journey—with Emma at your side, all the way, and all the time—to the *true you.*

—**Ramona Zabriskie,** Award-winning author of
Wife for Life: The Power to Succeed in Marriage,
Founder of Wife for Life University

INTRODUCTION

Most of us go through the same daily routines on automatic pilot. We get up, shower, grab a coffee, mumble cheerfully (or not) to the kids, feel guilty about not exercising (again) and commute to work. We see the same people on the train in the morning, sitting in the same seats and doing exactly the same things. Then, as an amorphous group, we rise from our seats at our destination and heave ourselves up the escalator, irritated that people are shoving and pushing, before the station building breathes us back out into the open air where we scatter in different directions.

Do you ever feel like you are drowning under the weight of modern life and never quite becoming that person that you know you are capable of being? Do you feel confident one day and full of self-doubt the next— like a pinball reacting to the highs and lows of the daily machine? Have you ever felt like you are living your life to fulfill someone else's dream? You thought that once you met the right guy, found the ideal job, got the new car, then you'd be happy, only to discover that the shadow settles over you again once the initial burst of joy has evaporated.

Perhaps you used to dream of being an astronaut, an opera singer or a ballet dancer, until you were told to make the dream a little smaller and more "realistic." You obediently narrowed your expectations, and you conformed to the rules, and here you are. At best, tomorrow will look exactly like today, and you will ride the highs and lows of life. At worst, you will never fill the void inside of you—not even with the things you buy, the vices you engage in or the love that you squeeze dry.

Do you often find that your relationships are complicated or that the emotional connection that you most crave is elusive? Do you feel like you give so much of yourself to others and get so little back? Do you cling to the belief that what others think of you is more important than your own approval and bend yourself out of shape to meet those exacting standards?

It doesn't have to be like this. Most of us have been looking for meaning in the wrong places for all these years, searching outside ourselves for fulfillment, when the ember has been burning inside us all along. It's still there; the light that we were born with—the one that faded slowly as we struggled through the growing pains toward adulthood.

Leading the Relationship with Yourself

When you live your life on autopilot, you are at the mercy of your subconscious programming. You think without thinking, and the thoughts that comprise your "software" are simply the legacy of your upbringing. It's time to take control—to lead your life consciously and deliberately as an expression of who you authentically are. That requires you to be keenly aware of your thinking, and if that thinking no longer serves you, then you can make the deliberate choice to overwrite the software. By "taking the lead" in your life, rather than following your programming, you are leading the relationship with *yourself*. That you could have a "relationship" with your own self might initially sound odd. You might think of "having a relationship" as connecting with another person who is separate from yourself. However, when you consciously connect with your authentic inner voice, you are able to listen carefully to the direction you truly wish to take in life. Rather than be a follower of your conditioning, you can lead the connection consciously with your authentic self and deliberately develop thinking that will enable you to be the best of which you are capable. That is what leading the relationship with your authentic self is all about.

When you lead in the relationship with yourself, your life is changed forever, and your daily routines become a journey of adventure where you experience genuine wonder at what unfolds before you. By leading a relationship with yourself, you are able to find true wellness, calm, confidence and energy. From that place, you can take the lead in your relationships with others. You come to understand that your existence is infectious; your smile radiates warmth and pulls laughter from others, your compassion drives you to understand instead of to judge. You are able to find the right words in the right tone at the right time to infuse every relationship with light. You can be present because you understand that that's all there is, and that leaves you free to enjoy every single moment. Your presence is your charisma—your magnetism that attracts others to you. As a leader, you will find that you can effortlessly inspire because you instinctively know how to "be" around those that need you. As a lover, you will disengage from the power battle and engage in being clear about what you need, being free to serve, support and love. As a friend, you can give—and take—and laugh and cry easily. When you lead the relationship with yourself, you are truly alive, and you take full responsibility for making every connection all that it can be—especially the connection that you create within yourself.

Relationships at Work

In a work context, relationships are a predictable indicator of success. Your parents may have enjoyed a career with one employer, but these days, your own expectations and the demands made of you are likely to be entirely different. The pace of life is faster, and the drive for commercial efficiency is greater than ever before. You may be looking for flexibility because you know that, in the age of technology, it is achievable in almost any job. You can work from home, from the office or from the beach. Job security has reduced, while employment flexibility has increased. You are likely to have several "careers" over the course of your working life and a greater opportunity than ever before to find work that gives your life meaning.

In the past, most of our communication took place face-to-face, within the construct of a hierarchical organization. The "tell culture" prevailed, and relationship dynamics were relatively fixed. Now, those who are effective communicators and relationship builders have an opportunity to stand out from the crowd. Successful relationships are key because clients are no longer bound by the constraints of loyalty to stay with you; they will go where the trust and the good deal are. Good deals can be matched, but trust has to be earned, and that's a tricky thing to do quickly. Great relationships with colleagues at work are critical to getting a job well done and swiftly while keeping the client happy. Our working environment is made up of people from Generations X, Y, Z and baby boomers, who all value different things and see the world in different ways, yet have to build close relationships across the decades to enable a business to run smoothly. Email is your friend when you want speed and efficiency, yet often your enemy—unless you understand how to use it well—when you want to be fully understood or build a great relationship dynamic. You know that if your boss rates you highly, you're moving upward, and if she doesn't, you're moving onward. You need to know how to positively influence your boss and ensure that you have a great connection with her.

Finding Your Purpose

As life speeds by, you may be asking yourself, "Is this all there is?" You may yearn to live a life of purpose, to make a contribution in your own unique way, but how do you identify what your purpose is? You may appreciate that, if you are clear about who you truly are and learn to live and work as your authentic self, you will be happy and much more effective, without having to waste your energy projecting yourself inauthentically to the world. Being your authentic self, finding meaning in what you do and identifying a life of purpose is within your grasp. From that place of confidence about your identity and your direction of travel, you then don't need to "feed" off your interactions with others. Instead, you can relax and focus your energy on enhancing the relationship so that you get the best out of your lover, your friends, your children and your boss (if you still have one!) while enjoying the fulfillment that great relationships provide.

When you are clear about your personal needs and your purpose, you become more resilient and able to give the best of yourself to motivate, engage and influence others. You are able to powerfully enhance all your relationships at work—and at home. You will no longer be "using" the relationship to gain power or exert your ego, because you are at peace and on purpose. You will be able to make quick decisions based on what's important to you, to recognize where you fit in and where you could better fulfill your potential. When change is imposed on you, you will be able see the opportunity in the change and capitalize on it. Your clarity and drive will help you to overcome every obstacle and provide you with the certainty of knowing that you have been the best of which you are capable—every day.

Life is moving faster than ever before, and distractions exist everywhere. Even time itself is rushed. You may constantly feel that you need to do more, be more, have more. Now is the time to take back control over who you authentically are, to light your internal torch, to ignite your personal potential and fire up your relationships. You can step out of the frame of reference that has been hemming you in, and breathe out. You have lived unconsciously according to the rules that others made for you for long enough. Aren't you tired of feeling empty, stressed and separate from everyone around you? It's time to change and grow.

My Own Story

When I began working as a lawyer, my sense of self-worth and confidence were entirely bound up in and dependent on the approval of others. I spent a lot of time and energy hiding my faults and trying to emphasize my strengths, bending myself out of shape in the process. I attempted to change with my immediate environment, like a chameleon. It was exhausting.

One Tuesday afternoon, I sat in my car looking through the windshield out at a brick wall. I felt a gaping hole inside me, and a lump in my throat began to rise as my body was wracked with sobs, but no tears came. I had cried them all out over the preceding months. I felt empty and hopeless. Not *hopeless* in the way you hear people glibly using the word, but quite literally, without any hope at all. Yet from the outside, my life must have looked pretty good. Okay, my marriage had failed somewhat spectacularly—though I had been too proud to tell even my closest friends that it had been withering slowly from a very unpromising start. My life was textbook; I had a great career, the house, the car, the clothes—all the trappings of "success." Yet, I felt the urge to just press the accelerator and let the car roar through that brick parapet and over the edge of the multistory car park. I knew I wouldn't do it.

I also understood that I had to do something. I was on antidepressant medication to get "well," but I instinctively felt that there must be another way to find some meaning within this mess.

Some weeks later, through the fog came the determination to start "fixing" whatever was "wrong" with me. I signed up for my first personal development course and glimpsed of a world of possibility. I became obsessive about learning how my mind and brain worked; I read book after book. I replaced my inner critic with an inner voice of compassion. I would turn to that compassionate and wise voice whenever I heard my inner critic snidely point out what a mess my life was, or whenever I felt stuck or overwhelmed. I imagined that my empowered, compassionate self was consciously taking control and leading me in the direction of a life that was more authentic. I realized that I had been blindly following my conditioning in whatever direction it had been leading—and it had led me to that dark place. I began to feel a tiny sense of calm—something that I had never felt before. I was truly like a phoenix rising from the ashes of despair, as if, all along, there had been the "authentic me" inside and who was making an appearance for the first time in my life. I no longer felt overwhelmed and stressed most of the time, even though I had felt that way for as long as I could remember. I had been trying to prove—subconsciously of course—that I was lovable. I had thought that I could only be lovable if I was perfect. I had worked hard to gain recognition, had made as many friends as I could because the more friends I had, the better a person I must be—right? I showed my friends and colleagues only the part of me that I thought they might like and accept, keeping my genuine, vulnerable self concealed. I had been inauthentic all my life, afraid that if people really knew me, they'd reject me.

As I consciously developed a relationship with myself, I became more aware of old programming that had kept me stuck in overwhelm and stress, and I released it, selecting instead thinking habits that felt more authentically like who I was and who I wanted to become. I moved from believing that the world was harsh and difficult to seeing that people were doing the best they could with what they had. I went from being sure that I was unlovable to believing that I was worthy of being loved unconditionally—but that had to start with loving and accepting myself. My daily work included visualization and, eventually, meditation. Visualization and the inner compassionate voice of my authentic self were the changes in my thinking that really turned things around for me. I became less judgmental and much more loving and accepting toward others. I began to notice some of my old operating patterns in others: the fear of rejection, the self-imposed pressure of seeking approval and the worry about not being good enough. I also became aware that those perspectives caused others to respond in ways that weren't helpful to the relationship dynamic. So, I played around with that and realized that my behavior could alter a relationship dynamic relatively quickly—but my behavior had to be an authentic result of my habitual-thinking patterns about others. I therefore began to focus not just on how I saw myself, but also on what was really going on beneath the "shell" of others and what the potential in a particular relationship might be. My life transformed in eighteen short months from the pit of hopelessness that I touched on in the multistory car park to a world of possibility where I understood that my inner experience was entirely created by what I choose to think, and therefore feel, about my outer experiences. I learned that life could be calm and stress-free, even though nothing had apparently changed on the outside, because I was consciously leading the most important relationship in my life—the one with myself. In turn, I understood the symbiotic nature of outer relationships; I could alter the dynamic simply by changing my thinking and how I felt about the potential of that relationship. For the first time in my life, I felt truly happy and content. I achieved more with less effort; I had insights and bursts of creativity that were new to me, and my relationships flourished.

I applied all that I was learning about what makes a great relationship to my leadership role with my team and to my relationship role with my clients. I found that the "joy factor" in my job increased overnight. I had gone from feeling like a square peg in a round hole to finding meaning in my work. I became passionate about finding my purpose, and realized that I had already stumbled across work that gave me meaning by making a difference to the lives of others through my relationships with them.

I began listening to my instinct to live a life that would be meaningful to me rather than one that would meet the approval of others. I left a successful career in law to pursue my passions. I remember a conversation with a very well-regarded and prominent lawyer around that time, who told me that he thought I was making a grave error—didn't I realize that I had a great career that others envied? I recognized, as he spoke, that he was applying his own values and priorities to my choice; that's why it made no sense to him. But his life would not fit me, just as my decision didn't suit him. Something had changed forever; I'd had a glimpse, for the first time in my life, of what truly gave me meaning. There was no going back.

It's hard for me today to imagine the hollowness of my old existence when I feel the richness of life as it is now. Once I understood that everything I was experiencing—my relationships, my sense of worth, the idea of who I was entitled to become—had been created by my limited thinking, I realized that the change I had been waiting for was *me*. Or more accurately, the "consciously aware" me who took the lead in transforming her limited thinking to inspiring dreams of who I was capable of becoming. I learned how to build new ways of seeing myself, and my potential, and how to build desire to follow through on even the most challenging of goals. I developed a process for building habitual thinking so that I would ritualize my new view of the world, of what I could achieve and how I could develop remarkable relationships. Once I had a taste for the freedom and joy it gave me, I developed more radical thinking. The formula has delivered me to a life of adventure, passion and purpose. I am happier beyond my wildest dreams. I have connections that nourish me, and I feel blessed. I understand how important it is for me to take the responsibility for leading in every relationship—especially the one with myself—because I know that, when I am clear about who I authentically am, my intention is to positively feed the symbiosis and change the dynamic and, therefore, what I experience from the other person. Life has become an adventure without limits.

This Approach Will Work for You Too

I have worked with many hundreds of leaders, managers, teachers, CEO's, health care professionals, lawyers, accountants, call center workers and others, who have experienced the revelation of understanding that *they* are the change they have been waiting for. They have embraced the techniques for leading a relationship with themselves and have gained a realization that we are capable of a life of meaning beyond our wildest (preprogrammed) dreams.

Never before has this realization been so precious, because our flexible and fast moving world has made the "box" almost disappear so that thinking outside of it is just about making new plans. Relationships remain at the heart of what gives us joy and at the soul of what makes a meaningful life. Those who learn how to lead relationship dynamics will have the edge over those who are still waiting for others to change. Those who can see that consciously selected, habitual thinking is the currency that will buy them the life and work of their dreams will leave confused colleagues, friends and family—who still believe that the "rules" must be obeyed—in their wake.

If you want to step out of the box—and into your limitless potential—to understand how to lead a relationship with yourself, build remarkable relationships with others, and feel the excitement of life pulsing through your veins, then get ready to push the walls of your current thinking away. You will need only a few things on this journey: a strong desire to be the best of which you are capable, the discipline to ritualize the new thinking that will get you there and the compassion to support others in their relationship with you. If you have those components, then you will be one of the few who can navigate the pressures of life easily and joyfully while others continue to take the same seat on the same train, thinking the same thoughts as yesterday.

Once you are clear about who you authentically are and what gives your life meaning, then you become independent of the good opinion of others. You inhabit a mind that is clear about life's priorities and does not need to "feed" off the energy of others. Instead, your need to make a contribution drives you to become the leader of all your relationships, doing what you can to allow the dynamic in each relationship to be as good as it possibly can be. You feel empowered to influence others positively, choosing resourceful responses, minimizing your own and others' stress and enabling others to fulfill their potential.

Once you begin to put the steps contained in this book in to action, you will notice immediate change. You will encounter a personal transformation from stress to calm, from anxiety to confidence and from weariness to boundless energy. You will have clarity of purpose, feel empowered, self-assured and clear about how to transform difficult relations into healthy and mutually fulfilling relationships. You will be inspired to shift those interactions that you find caustic to a level of engagement that you feel is comfortable, with compassion and empathy for the other person.

How This Book Is Set Out

Part one of this book focuses on the tools and techniques for leading the relationship with yourself. It provides insight into why life may have been feeling like a struggle for so long, how to overcome that struggle and dance with life by developing your own thinking patterns and sets out an inspiring vision for what life will be like when you lead in the relationship with yourself. It also sets out a practical process for establishing your purpose and living a life of meaning. If you choose to accept it, a thirty-day challenge is included that will enable you to get to work right away by building empowering thinking habits.

In part two, you will see how you have been "following" in your relationship with others, and you will discover the possibilities for building powerful relationships by taking the lead. There is practical guidance for developing a "leading relationship mind-set" and the skills required for forging deeper relationships and having those difficult conversations. Finally, I have developed a set of six *resilience factors* that will enable you to work out why a relationship is not functioning and what you can do to improve the dynamic immediately. I have also set you a further thirty-day challenge to enable you to start work straight away on building powerful positive dynamics in any relationship. Finally, the appendix sets out some practical visualization exercises that will help you lead a relationship with yourself and with others.

PART ONE

LEADING THE RELATIONSHIP WITH YOURSELF

CHAPTER 1

THE PINBALL IN THE MACHINE

"Our life is what our thoughts make of it."
—**Marcus Aurelius**

Recognizing Your Own Thoughts and Thought Patterns

What is *Thinking*?

According to a 2010 Harvard research paper, our minds are lost in thought, on average, 47 percent of the time.[1] That means that we are lost in our thinking for almost half of our lifetime—and we are not even aware of it! We think about what happened in the past, what might happen in the future, what he might be thinking, whether it's raining outside and that you probably shouldn't have said what you did to your boss. We have a constant running internal commentary going on in our minds: judging, reliving, worrying, lambasting, rehearsing, self-deprecating. In fact, research has also shown that 65 percent of our thoughts are negative and/or redundant, so not only are we lost in thought, we are also wasting our time and making ourselves feel bad in the bargain![2] As the researchers from Harvard said, "A human mind is a wandering mind, and a wandering mind is an unhappy mind. The ability to think about what is not happening is a cognitive achievement that comes at an emotional cost."[3]

What Are *Thought Patterns*?

It's been rumored that we have between 60,000 and 70,000 thoughts per day, though those figures do vary. However, the figure that is consistently accepted is that 90 percent of the thoughts that you have today will be the same as the thoughts that you had yesterday.[4] If we stick to a figure of 60,000 thoughts per day, then you are going to have 54,000 thoughts tomorrow that are the same as the ones that you have today. To put it another way, 90 percent of the stories you tell yourself today will be the same as the stories you told yourself yesterday. Just think about that for a second—and you may well think about it tomorrow and the day after that too! These repetitious thoughts are called *thinking patterns* and arise from our *core beliefs*— those things we believe to be true about ourselves and the world around us. We are often not consciously aware of what our specific core beliefs are until we start to notice the repeated thoughts that arise in response to certain situations that we are faced with. Until we consciously question whether that thinking is really true or is serving in our growth, we will stick rigidly to it, and it will be the "filter" through which we assess our experiences.

What Thoughts Do You "Dwell On" and Follow Most Frequently?
Once you start to notice the content of the running commentary in your mind, you will begin to identify the thinking patterns that tend to take up the most space. For example, whenever you are facing a challenge such as delivering a presentation or meeting a group of new people, your internal commentary will take off in a particular direction, and your emotions—and normally the end result—will neatly follow. In the case of a presentation, your thoughts may be fear based—fear of failure by boring the audience, "drying up" or being unable to answer a question posed by a member of the audience. Every time you contemplate preparing for the presentation, that commentary will run and gather momentum. That will probably lead to procrastination and a last minute, rushed preparation of the presentation. You know you haven't done your best in the preparation and that makes the prospect of delivering it even more terrifying. Sweaty palms, dry mouth, "sponge brain" are the natural physiological responses to your thinking as your stand up in front of your audience in "fight or flight" mode.

If you find that you feel constantly stressed about your workload (at home and at work), you can bet that there is a thinking pattern that causes you to rehearse the same thought-emotion cycle every time you contemplate what you have to get through. You may struggle sticking with diets or fitness regimes, and again, there will be a thinking pattern sitting behind that inner battle that keeps you stuck in the cycle of "try-struggle-fail-what's the point?" Or perhaps you worry about what other people are thinking of you and often feel self-conscious when in the company of others, concerned that what you say will evoke negative judgments. You may constantly strive for perfection because only the best is good enough. Perhaps you aim low because of fear of failure. Whatever your particular worry, fear or concern, you can be sure that, through your thinking, you are cultivating its continued hold over you. Your thoughts are taking you in precisely the direction that you would least choose to follow if you felt that you were in complete control, if you felt that you could forge a more constructive path by leading your thinking rather than your thinking leading you, and therefore by leading a relationship with yourself.

The Leading Nature of Our Thinking— and Our Tendency to Blindly Follow

Thoughts are neurons that string into place and create the "chemical" of emotion. Every time you have a thought, in addition to making neurotransmitters, your brain also makes another chemical called a *neuropeptide* that sends a message to your body. Your body then reacts by having a feeling. The brain picks up that the body is having a feeling and so generates another thought matched directly to that feeling. That will produce more of the same chemical messages that allow you to think the way you were just feeling. This could give rise to a vicious cycle, or a virtuous cycle depending on how empowering or otherwise the originating thought was. If you think of something neutral, like a cloud, you may find that there's really no emotion arising as a result of that thought. But leave your mind to its own devices, and it will conjure up a memory of an experience in the past to do with clouds, and within moments, you will be feeling an emotion: joy or sadness, anger or happiness, regret or longing. Our brain is wired that way. Every thought generates an emotion, and that feeling will link to a thought, and so the cycle continues. Before you know it, you've been ruminating for eleven minutes on an event from your past while sitting behind the steering wheel of your car and have no recollection of the last three miles of your journey. Does that sound familiar? Your emotions feel as intense as when you first felt them during the experience that you are thinking of. Your physiology, too, has obeyed the command and is sending adrenalin to help you during the imagined imminent "attack." Most of us go about our daily lives reliving memories from the past or worrying about what will happen in the future, and we keenly feel the emotions that link to those memories or imaginings. Our thoughts lead us, and we blindly follow, relinquishing all control over our emotions and the direction of that moment. As life is simply a series of connected moments, we fail to lead much of the direction that our life is taking.

Common Thinking Patterns

In my coaching practice, I find that the two most common core beliefs that lie behind thinking patterns that lead my clients to more of the same pain they want to avoid are variants of "I am unlovable" and "I am not good enough." Obviously, my clients do not enter the room, wailing these words—in fact, they are blissfully unaware that they are simply following thinking patterns that keep ensuring the same (unwanted) results. Sometimes, it isn't necessary for us to explore the core beliefs that are giving rise to the repetitive thinking—simply working on the thinking patterns themselves will achieve remarkable results. On those occasions when it has been appropriate to explore the core belief, naming it has been like "turning a light on," and realizing the truth of the core belief for the individual—whether one of the two I named above, or another—has been a stark reality. In fact, tears invariably accompany the recognition of the belief and how it has been leading the direction of their lives and their relationships with themselves for decades. In working through the steps of this book, it might be useful to loosely keep in mind the two common core beliefs, just to see if they may be true for you. However, in most cases, it simply isn't necessary to go to those depths—but rather simply to focus on what thinking patterns you have been following.

So, What Are Yours?

At this stage, it would be unusual for you to have a revelation as to what your thinking patterns are. But I expect that you are starting to listen more consciously to the running commentary in your head and will already be aware of some of the themes that have been "leading" your perception of "who you are" and what you are capable of. The first step is to gently notice what your thoughts are, what pattern or "themes" they follow and to regard them with interest in terms of how often they recur, how you feel when they do and whether they are leading you in a positive or negative direction. Don't worry about defending the "truthfulness" of them by looking for evidence to support them—your instinct will be to do that, and I would ask you to resist that instinct at all costs.

Where Do Your Thought Patterns Come From?

We Are All in the Same Boat

The way that we are "wired" means that all of us are in the same boat—we follow the lead of our thinking, without thinking, most of the time. In order to build the desire to take the lead in our relationship with ourselves, by *leading* our thinking, it might help to understand a little about how the brain and mind work and where our existing thought patterns have come from.

The Science Bit

First of all, let's look at some of the mechanics of the brain. The *limbic system* is the part of the brain that carries out three key functions: sensing emotion, making and storing memories and generating arousal. The limbic system could be described as the "feeling and reacting brain" which is interposed between the "thinking brain" and the output mechanisms of the nervous system. The two *amygdalae* in our brain assist in the production of memories—particularly as they relate to emotional events and emergencies—the development of the fear emotion and also play a major role in pleasure and sexual arousal. The amygdalae are also responsible for selecting which memories are stored and where—based on how huge an emotional response a particular event evokes.

Somewhere between 1 and 5 percent of our brain's processing power is used by our conscious mind. The remainder—up to 99 percent— is used by our subconscious, unconscious, autonomic and automatic systems. The automatic and autonomic systems mean that we don't consciously have to think about how to breathe, make our heart beat or digest our food; all that is done on automatic pilot. The greatest part of our brain is occupied by our subconscious mind, and studies have consistently shown that most of our decisions, actions, emotions and behaviors are generated by the 95 percent or so of our brain activity that is beyond our conscious awareness—that means that at least 95 percent of our life is driven by the programming in our subconscious mind. The power of our subconscious is around a million times greater than our conscious mind, and our brains begin to prepare for action just over a third of a second before we consciously decide to act. Accordingly, even when we "think" we are conscious, it's our subconscious mind that is actually making our decisions for us.

Our brain is a "truth-seeking device"—it is the job of the subconscious to create our reality according to our "internal programming" in order to demonstrate that our current thinking is "true," and to ignore or rationalize any evidence that might contradict the "story" that we are telling ourselves.

The subconscious mind begins to operate prebirth, while the conscious mind begins its development at around the age of three. We therefore function without the effective "filter" of our conscious mind in our early stages of development. That means that our subconscious mind develops in the absence of our mature and conscious mind; and therefore, our ability to qualify or rationalize negative programming is absent during those early years, including during our "emotional development window."

Our conscious mind controls our voluntary functions but is able to do only one thing at a time. If you want to carry out two activities simultaneously, then that is only possible when one of them is handed over to the subconscious mind while you focus consciously on carrying out the other. Activities such as driving a car become effortless only because the elements of that activity are relegated to our subconscious mind. An exercise such as simultaneously rubbing your stomach and patting your head is only possible if you relegate one action to your subconscious mind. To put it another way, you start rubbing your stomach and then stop consciously thinking about that action before you start patting your head. I bet you're trying it now!

The way we are "wired" is to develop this tremendous resource, called our subconscious mind, that takes all the effort out of life by "ritualizing" thinking and doing habits so that we don't have to trouble our conscious mind with focusing on those repetitive thoughts about who we are and what we are capable of, or tasks such as tying our shoelaces. The downside (and it's a huge one) is that when we ritualize thinking that is disempowering, we are blissfully unaware that it's even there—holding us back—while also preventing us from "waking up" and leading a relationship with ourselves by engaging our conscious mind.

The Development Process

As children, our brains begin as a "jumble of neurons." Every input from each of the five senses then starts to form "programs" in our brain. It's critical that these programs are established at the appropriate stage of development, because there is a "time window" for doing so; after the window closes, programming limits are set up that are difficult to overcome. While some of the neurons have already been hardwired by the genes fertilized in the egg, they are related to the breathing, heartbeat and reflex functions. It's the trillions and trillions of remaining neurons that are like unprogrammed software with infinite potential. If the neurons are used, then they become integrated into the circuitry of the brain; but if they are not used, they may die. It is the experiences of your childhood that determine which neurons are used, just like a programmer reconfigures the circuits on a computer. The experiences that you have had as a child determine whether you grow up to be confident or shy, expressive or dull, intelligent or otherwise.[5]

Our early experiences therefore significantly determine how we "turn out," depending on what stimuli we have been exposed to—or not exposed to— within the relevant development "window." By the age of six, we have learned how to seek approval and adapt our behavior in certain circumstances as part of our subconscious conditioning. We have already received thousands of messages, spoken and unspoken, which our subconscious mind has absorbed literally without the benefit of rational processing. In short, as a result of our development process, we have acquired thinking patterns, conditioned reflexes and concepts relating to ourselves and to our environment that we are not consciously aware of.

Thinking patterns are formed by a series of neurons establishing a chain set up in our brain tissue. That chain represents a "shortcut" so that an association is formed effortlessly between an event and a conclusion: "Unless I am perfect, I am unlovable" or "I am not good enough" are examples of the core beliefs that can arise as a consequence of the associations that have been formed. Because many of our core beliefs are programmed at an early age, we are not consciously aware of them.

The result of all this is that, as adults, we are likely to have many negative thinking patterns in our subconscious mind that were developed prior to our twentieth birthday. Those may have been planted unwittingly by well-meaning parents, caregivers, relatives, teachers or friends, or by a childhood rejection or a thoughtless threat that made us feel exceptionally vulnerable. For example, if you were told throughout your childhood that you were a capable, lovable individual, and you received positive emotional signals and were highly attuned during your emotional development window, you are likely to have a broader and more constructive emotional repertoire. If you were "told," either expressly or implicitly that you were worthless and would never amount to anything, then those kinds of signals color your assumptions about yourself and predispose you toward negative thinking patterns, especially if your positive emotions were not attuned during the emotional development window. Either way, you will have developed a host of thinking patterns associated with your way of seeing yourself, others and the world. I don't want to lay all this at our parents' door however; they are a product of their upbringing, just as we are a product of ours, and in many cases, they were doing the best they could, based on what they believed.

These thinking patterns or beliefs are thoughts that you hold to be true to the extent that you no longer question them. You may believe that the world is a hostile place or that people can't be trusted. Alternatively, you may credit everyone with doing the best they can with what they have. Whatever your beliefs, your brain will do what it can to see the world in a way that is consistent with those beliefs. In short, that means that your subconscious thinking is leading the direction of your life and your relationships— particularly the one you have with yourself. If you want to increase your confidence, self-esteem, sense of calm and self-belief, then choosing to consciously lead your thinking is a great place to start. In fact, nothing will change unless you begin to lead the relationship with yourself.

How Do Your Thinking Patterns Affect You?

They Keep You Stuck

By now, I hope you've come to terms with the fact that you have a collection of thinking patterns in your subconscious mind that are triggered by external events. When the trigger activates, your neurons fire to produce the chemical of emotion, and your running commentary continues to lead you in that same old mental direction. Your emotions trigger more thoughts of the same flavor as the one that was initially triggered, and your actions and behavior obediently display the consequences of your thinking.

My coaching clients often come to me with a particular problem; they may have an interview coming up which is really important to them, and they want to make sure that they don't crash and burn in a sea of nerves like they normally do. They perhaps want to change career and overcome the fear that has paralyzed them for years from making the break. Or, they want to have more fulfilling and meaningful relationships. Whatever the transformation sought, the answer always begins in the same place: how they lead the relationship with themselves through the conscious management of their thinking. By focusing on a particular problem, or attempting to change a particular area of their lives, they are enabled to see the relevant thinking pattern that has been keeping them stuck.

Gregor consulted me about shifting his thinking regarding money. He was brought up in a loving family, where he lacked nothing, but only because of his mother's frugality. He therefore understood the importance of being prudent and still felt the perpetual fear that at any moment there might "not be enough." His default thinking when he and his wife were making purchasing decisions was always that there wouldn't be enough—regardless of how much money was in their bank account. This had caused many arguments between them. His marriage was, quite literally, dependent on him being able to change his attitude toward spending money. When Gregor consulted me, he had no awareness that his thinking was hooked to his past experiences relating to money when he was growing up. His first impulse was to justify why what he thought was true, and we talked about what would happen if he clung to the old "story"; his desire to change had to trump his desire to be "right." Once he understood the origins of his thinking patterns about money and how he could develop new thinking patterns, coupled with his real incentive to change his thinking in order to achieve marital bliss, he set to work on consciously being aware of his thinking, and then choosing different thinking which was logically based on funds available rather than the subconscious fear of lack.

They Act as Self-Fulfilling Prophecies

We tend to get exactly what we expect when we blindly follow our programmed thinking; it causes us to self-sabotage so that we fulfill our expected potential. What if we took the conscious decision to lead the relationship with ourselves: To see ourselves as the children we once were, with all the programming that now no longer serves us, and to take charge, as the adults we now are, to forge new inner mental pathways that enable us to lead our lives rather than follow our outdated thinking?

Susan was convinced that she was just a "sensitive person" and would have to go through life suffering the slings and arrows of outrageous fortune more acutely than the rest of us. That was until she realized that thinking she was a sensitive person was driving a set of habitual responses that would fit with that self-identity whenever something happened about which she "should" feel a sense of hurt or betrayal. In fact, Susan was on the lookout for things to feel sensitive about—her antennae twitching constantly whenever she picked up a sensitizing signal. She even sat like a sensitive person; her body held closed, head down, subconsciously protecting herself from the inevitable attacks that were going to be directed at her. Other people treated Susan as if she was a sensitive person. They were subconsciously responding to what they saw in the way she expressed herself physically and what they heard when she expressed herself verbally. During one of our sessions, she told me how relieved she felt that she wasn't really exceptionally "sensitive"—she just thought that she was. She realized that she had freed herself from the lifetime of suffering she had always believed was ahead of her because of her "sensitivity." She began to tell a new, more empowering story of who she was. She chose to believe that she was capable, that her own approval was more important than the opinion of others and that, anyway, their opinion was likely to be infected by their own self-identity. That newly developed trust in her own opinion and her consciously chosen empowering thinking helped build her confidence and, inevitably, changed her outcomes because when we believe we can, we try harder, we overcome difficulties more readily and we achieve greater results from our endeavors.

> *"We do not see things as they are; we see them as we are."*
> —the **Talmud**

Forging a New Inner Mental Pathway—Leading the Relationship with Your Authentic Self

The first task that I gave you earlier in this book was to simply notice your thinking but not to try to defend its veracity. I held you back from the temptation to defend your current thinking patterns because I wanted you to understand that much of what you think over and over again is linked to beliefs that are no longer relevant to who you are now. The first and most important task remains that of objectively noticing your thinking, without judgment and with compassion, and understanding that it is a result of what you had to do to relish experiences or endure and survive challenges. However, the way in which we are best able to "tune in" to our thinking will vary depending upon how our brain operates—in terms of its "sensory preferences." The field of neuro-linguistic programming identifies these preferences as visual, auditory and kinesthetic. Those whose dominant sensory preference is visual will organize their thoughts and learn best via pictures. Those who are auditory will communicate using words that have to do with the auditory system; and those whose preference is kinesthetic will communicate by using words related to feelings. In terms of identifying what our existing thinking patterns are, those with an auditory sensory preference will be able to identify thinking patterns most easily through listening to their thoughts—usually by way of consciously noticing their inner dialogue. Those who are visual will be able to "watch" their thinking—much like a ticker tape that runs along the bottom of a television screen, broadcasting the latest news headlines. That analogy is particularly helpful to those of us who are visual by dominance (as most of us are), because we can see that image in our mind's eye. For those whose sensory preference is kinesthetic, they will have a high level of emotional awareness; and how they feel is therefore likely to sound the initial "alarm" that some unhelpful subconscious thinking is going on. If you are not sure what your sensory preference is, there's a lot of information available on the topic and assessment tools for you to find out, and I recommend taking the time to do that.

Be Honest with Yourself

The appreciation that "you are not your thinking" can be life changing if you allow it to sink in to your soul. It's a huge leap for most of us to begin to accept that we cannot believe everything we think and, indeed, that being consciously speculative about what we choose to believe will open us up to a world where we can lead a relationship with ourselves and thereby learn to think differently and consciously about who we authentically are and what we want to achieve in life. It takes a lot of work and attention to see your "inner self" as distinct from your outer experiences, and to lead an internal relationship that involves checking your thinking, choosing your mental direction and forging a mental pathway that is empowering. It would be much easier to sit back, believe your thinking and tell yourself that you can't change what happens in life. But in the end, when it's too late to lead in each of those moments that counted toward the sum total of who you became, you may just regret failing to lead the relationship with yourself by developing empowering thinking habits. Make this moment the start of taking charge of the new direction in your life so that you can look back, in years to come, with a sense of pride that you had the courage to start building your own subconscious powerhouse.

It's Time to Stop Being the Pinball in the Machine

Take a moment to reflect now on those thinking patterns that have been dictating how you respond—day in, day out—and on the thoughts that have determined how you feel about yourself and how you think the world feels about you. If there is any sense of unease in that reflection, good news does lie ahead. It's possible to develop the only habit that matters—the habit of leading the relationship with yourself so that you can stop being the pinball in the machine.

CHAPTER 2

HABITS THAT WILL ENABLE YOU TO LEAD IN THE RELATIONSHIP WITH YOURSELF

"Motivation is what gets you started. Habit is what keeps you going."

—Jim Ryun

Why Habits Are So Powerful

What Are Habits?

Habits are sequences of actions that are learned progressively and performed unconsciously. The process of developing habits is known as *ritualization* or *automaticity*. In his book *The Power of Habit*, Charles

19

Duhigg discusses a study involving mice in a cheese maze. The first time the mice were put into a particular maze, their brain activity was robust and intense; the mice sniffed and clawed the walls analyzing every part of the maze as they raced through it to find the cheese at the end. If the mice were put in the same maze day after day, they found the cheese faster, but their overall brain activity decreased. The mice had ritualized the process of finding the cheese.

In the same way, when we ritualize any process (such as tying our shoelaces), a tiny part of our brain called the *basal ganglia* takes over a series of actions so that we no longer have to actively concentrate. Accordingly, once we have developed the new mental habit, we use little or no willpower to think the empowering thought. Choosing to think that you *are capable of whatever you put your mind to*, and developing that into a *habitual*-thinking pattern—that your subconscious mind will therefore look for evidence to prove right— will determine what you notice and feel, how you behave and project yourself, and the actions that you take. The action or behavior that flows from the (now subconscious) thought happens unconsciously or requires only the smallest depletion of our willpower, all because we have developed a new subconscious program. That lies at the heart of leading a relationship with yourself.

Leading Yourself to Become the Best of Which You Are Capable

John Wooden, former UCLA basketball coach defined *success* as "the peace of mind attained from attempting to do the best of which you are capable." The truth is that you are already amazing, when you get out of your own way. The main restriction that applies to doing the best of which you are capable is your own set of preconceptions of what it is you are capable of. To challenge any limits you may have been applying subconsciously to the fulfillment of your own potential is a great place to start.

I want to adapt John Wooden's quote slightly. My definition of success is "the peace of mind attained from *being* the best of which you are capable." There are some simple ways of engaging your conscious mind to overcome unhelpful subconscious thinking patterns on a moment-to-moment basis so that you can be the best of which you are capable in the here and now. Happily, if you engage in those activities on a daily basis, they will develop into habits and become ritualized so that, habit by habit, the result will be a reprogramming of your subconscious mind to create positive habitual-thinking patterns that will enable you to be the best of which you are capable, every day of your life.

If thoughts lead to emotions, and emotions lead to action, then the most powerful habits to develop are "thinking" habits. Most often, we tend to focus on "doing" habits, like going to the gym three times a week or eating a healthy breakfast every morning. Those good intentions can quickly fade into obscurity because "doing" habits use up a lot of willpower, and willpower is a finite daily resource dependent on our blood glucose levels.

A study carried out in 2011 found that experienced parole judges in Israel granted freedom about 65 percent of the time to the first prisoner who appeared before them on a given day.[6] By the end of a morning session, other prisoners' chance of release had dropped to almost zero. After the same judge returned from a lunch break, the first prisoner once again had about a 65 percent chance of freedom. Once again, the odds declined steadily thereafter. The reason offered by the authors of the study for the disparity in fortunes of the prisoners is that making successive decisions depletes a limited mental facility, in the same way as successive press-ups wear out our deltoid muscles. As people get tired, they look for shortcuts, and one of the easiest shortcuts is to uphold the status quo. A way of reducing reliance on willpower is to develop new (empowering) habitual thinking that replaces any existing subconscious thinking patterns that may be unhelpful. Often, the reason that we default to our "factory settings"—in subconscious-mind terms—is that there is just too much going on in our lives, or we are stressed or too tired to remember to consciously choose to think a more empowering thought on every occasion when it would be helpful to do so. But if we choose some *core* thinking habits that we could ritualize so that they became part of our subconscious mind-set, then that would mean that we wouldn't have to engage our willpower every time. It's that focus on developing the core thinking habits that is the backbone of leading a strong relationship with yourself so that you can be the best of which you are capable.

The Neural Process for Creating a New Habitual Thought

An experiment carried out at Harvard Medical School involved volunteers who were asked to learn and practice a five-finger piano exercise.[7] The members of one group were instructed to play as fluidly as they could, trying to keep to the metronome's sixty beats per minute. Every day for five days, the volunteers practiced for two hours.

At the end of each day's practice session, the volunteers sat beneath a coil of wire that sent a brief magnetic pulse—via a strip running from the crown of the head toward each ear—into the motor cortex of their brains. The equipment mapped how much of the piano players' motor cortexes controlled the finger movements needed for the piano exercise. The scientists found that after only a week of practice, the stretch of motor cortex devoted to these finger movements took over surrounding areas. What this means to you and me, is that repeatedly performing a task enables neurons to fire and then wire together so that new neural pathways are quickly developed, and the "wiring" enables the automation of the thought or action. That automation process applies equally to habitual-thinking patterns as it does to physical tasks. That's partly why your subconscious thinking will repeat, as if on a loop system, at the rate of 90 percent day after day. You could dramatically alter the rate of positive progress in your life by consciously choosing to develop new neural pathways or habits. The forming of the new neural pathway is exactly like creating a path through a forest; what starts as footsteps on the fallen leaves develops into a well-worn and easily identifiable track as a result of the repeated footfalls. Repeatedly and consciously choosing a new way of thinking will become increasingly effortless as the "pathway" develops traction in your brain.

The Most Powerful Habits for Leading the Relationship with Yourself

Using the Science to Your Own Advantage

The statistics that I shared with you in chapter 1 are those that apply when we are not consciously choosing to operate our subconscious mind as a positive resource, but rather we are simply allowing old programming to run unchecked. The truth is that we only use around 10 percent of our subconscious-mind resources—excluding the autonomic and automatic systems. We allow old thinking patterns to run us, rather than choosing which beliefs to keep and which to replace so that we ritualize thinking patterns that enable us to fulfill our potential. There is in each of us an exciting opportunity to harness the resource of our subconscious mind.

The Habit of Thought Awareness

Thought awareness involves understanding, first of all, that you are not your thinking. Once you are able to cultivate the habit of detachment, then you can watch or listen to your thinking with an objective viewpoint and question whether it is helpful to follow that line of thinking, or whether you might choose to change your perspective about the situation and how you see your role in it. Developing this habit enables you to *ritualize* the detachment from your thinking and then instinctively and critically assess whether the line of thought is helpful or not. In this way, you consciously lead how you respond rather than subconsciously being led by the emotion that flows from the "faulty" thinking.

The Habit of Observing Your Inner Voice

Tuning in to your inner voice, observing your thoughts and being sensitized to your emotional state is a very powerful habit to cultivate. In the case of your inner voice, being able to notice, without judgment, what you say to yourself is an interesting exercise. You may find that your inner voice is frequently critical and that the criticisms are running along a theme. We are initially reluctant to believe that something we have allowed to run amok in our mind for most of our lives might be unhelpful; and therefore, we often try to rationalize how that voice is there for our own good. After all, for those perfectionists among us, it drives us on and encourages us to strive for something better. Doesn't it? That must be good for us, right?

Our inner voice is our "inner vice." It's familiar and comfortable. It often makes us feel inadequate or anxious, but we're hooked on its distorted view of reality. It's time to kick this habit. We've already looked at the first step to kicking it—observing it as if it's a stranger in our head. When we learn to listen with detachment and notice that the voice repeats the same messages over and over again, then we can see where some of those 54,000 repetitious thoughts are springing from, day after day. However, now that we are released from its grip, it's time to take the next step. That step involves replacing the unhelpful habitual thought patterns with some more helpful ones.

The good news is that we don't need to lie down on a couch and talk about our childhood so that we can understand where the core beliefs that are giving rise to the thought patterns came from. All we need to do is stop judging and start supporting ourselves. When the judgmental voice comes up, be amused. After all, it's only an old, outdated thought that hasn't kept up with who we now are. If we become irritated or frustrated with the judgmental voice, we are simply giving it gas. Let's save the gas for the replacement: productive or supportive thoughts. So, if we find ourselves in an important meeting, and our inner voice is ranting about how stupid our last comment or contribution to the meeting was, we should be amused. Replace the message with another more constructive message, such as "I might have been able to put that better. If I was to make another contribution on that point, what could I say that others would find useful?" Because the brain is a device that immediately goes off in the direction we send it, then it's likely to find an answer to that question for us. A question such as that one will keep us present in the meeting too. If we don't take conscious control, the judgmental voice will take our attention from the meeting to the filing cabinet full of memories of all the other occasions when we said something stupid. We will miss the discussion at the meeting and perhaps also the point at which we could have asked that vital question. Our subconscious mind reasons from the specific to the general. It will take us in a thought direction that makes us feel stupid over and over again—if we don't get our conscious mind engaged in replacing judgment with productive thought. In doing so, we take the lead in developing our conscious identity.

The Habit of Mindfulness
Mindfulness is about stepping back and seeing our thoughts clearly, rather than being lost in them. Focused relaxation allows thoughts to come and go without our active involvement. When I began to cultivate the practice of mindfulness, I noticed just how difficult it was initially to sustain the practice because, if I allowed my attention to lapse for a second, my mind would drift off in thought. However, I was determined to ritualize the habit.

Often, the easiest place to start is to observe your thoughts while doing a mundane task like laundry or driving. For example, while I was driving, I would notice the car in front of me—its brake lights, the trunk style—and I would pay attention to the road markings, traffic lights, the body posture of pedestrians as they crossed the road. Sometimes, my attention would drift off, and I would realize that my thoughts were negative and were taking me in a direction I simply did not want to follow. Recognizing that this was simply a thinking pattern, I would smile inwardly and gently redirect my mind back to the present moment. I understood that if I became frustrated or irritated by the direction my thoughts were taking—or that they were springing up at all—I would just be giving them power. It's sometimes helpful to think of negative thoughts as red balloons and to imagine letting them go as you watch them float off into the sky and out of sight. Jack Kornfield, author of *A Path with Heart*, compares thoughts that pop up during meditation to a puppy; you command it to stay, and it wanders off. You pick the puppy back up, place it in the same spot and instruct it to stay; but once again, the puppy wanders off. For a third time you command the puppy to stay, and it goes off into the corner and pees! The trick is to remain amused and keep picking up the puppy and commanding it to stay. Eventually it will learn.

Mindfulness is difficult to maintain when life gets busy, and the demands on your time are high. One thought that helps refocus my mind is that I am only able to do one thing at a time and, if I am mindful, I am more likely to do it well, and therefore not have to redo it or pick up the fallout from it having been badly done. Most importantly, I find that if I am able to maintain mindfulness, then my enjoyment of the experience increases dramatically; and the completion of a difficult task is rewarding. Even the actions we repeat every day could be imbued with greater joy and presence through the habit of mindfulness. Rather than running through your to-do list in the shower, you might choose to consciously enjoy the feeling of the warm water running over your skin, grateful for the luxury that evades so many less fortunate than you. You could consciously savor the licorice flavor of your coffee as you listen to the rippling giggles of your two-year-old daughter.

As we now know, our subconscious thinking will take precedence unless controlled and overridden by consciously made choices regarding what thoughts are helpful or constructive about our present and our future, and our past for that matter. If we don't consciously choose to enjoy and influence the present moment, we will be ambushed by memories from our past or anticipation of our future.

The Habit of Releasing Yourself from the Grip of Your Past

Often, the most powerful place to start is to choose thinking about our past in a way that enables us to release its grip on us. If thoughts of what went wrong in our past generate strong emotions, then we are reliving the past over and over again. If we are able to change our thinking about our history by choosing more constructive references, then we enable ourselves to move on and to free our mind for some fresh thinking. As someone close to me once said, "The best thing about the past is that it's, well, in the past."

The Habit of Creating Positive Expectations of Yourself

If you often feel overwhelmed by the volume of information that comes firing at you on a daily basis, it's no wonder; some sources say that every day we are exposed to somewhere between 70,000 and 110,000 stimuli. We are able to *consciously* notice only about 10 percent of that available information. The key question is: What aspect of our conscious or subconscious minds determines what to filter in and what to sift out? Our "filter" has its "factory settings": those subconscious thinking patterns that have been installed gradually over our lifetime. Those "settings" will determine what we notice and what we don't; the brain will "filter" in all the information that is consistent with your existing self-identity and fail to notice what is inconsistent with it. We will see the person in the front row looking at her BlackBerry during our presentation, but miss the man in the third row listening attentively, because we believe that we just aren't any good at public speaking. What we notice will trigger more of the same thinking that caused us to set that particular "filter" in the first place.

Studies have shown that our expectations of ourselves can be shaped by outside factors and impact on our performance unless we take conscious control. In a Canadian study carried out in 2006, 220 female students read fake research reports claiming that men had a 5 percent advantage over women in mathematics performance.[8] The group was divided in two, with one group reading that the advantage was due to recently discovered genetic factors, while the other group read that the advantage resulted from the way teachers stereotype girls and boys in elementary school—then the subjects were given a mathematics test. The women who had read that men have a genetic advantage scored lower than those who had read that men have an advantage due to stereotyping. When they were primed to think that the disadvantage was inevitable, the women performed as if they truly had that disadvantage. When we "prime" ourselves, through our thinking, to believe that we just don't have that talent or capability, then we block our ability to demonstrate it.

That we tend to get exactly what we focus on is largely due to a set of connected nuclei in the human brain, which help regulate attention, called the *reticular activating system* (RAS). During tasks that require particular alertness and attention, there is increased blood flow in this formation. Your RAS helps you to store and recall references, and while your prior experience is the most common reference point used by the RAS, consciously focusing on a new approach or objective will also act as a reference point. Let's think about this in a practical context; if you have ever bought a car that you've had your eye on for a while, your RAS was at work. Let's imagine that car was a BMW Z4. You loved the shape of that model and persuaded yourself that the two-seater setup wouldn't cause practical issues when the baby came along. You had set your heart on getting a decent secondhand one, with around 5,000 miles on the odometer and ideally in blue or silver. The initial focus on the make and model had you noticing BMW Z4s driving around all over the place. Then, once you narrowed your focus even more, you occasionally noticed some blue and silver ones. Had you not focused on that make and model of car, then chances are you wouldn't have noticed how many were on the road. The same applies to any area of focus in life; when you plan to sell or buy a house, it's only then that you notice real estate agents' advertisements all over the place and a huge number of "For Sale" signs on your street. If you have become pregnant, then your conscious attention will be bombarded with baby-related paraphernalia.

If you get more of what you focus on, then leading in the relationship with yourself by developing the habit of expecting the best from yourself in any situation will "switch" your filter to a positive setting.

The Four-Stage Habit-Forming Process

The Four Stages to Creating
Empowering Habitual-Thinking Patterns

Developing empowering thinking habits is what lies at the heart of leading a relationship with yourself. It takes self-discipline and perseverance to develop a new habit, and it's helpful to have a process to work through and an understanding of how long that process is likely to take. I've set out a four-stage habit-forming process that will ensure that every new empowering thought that you want to ritualize will stick.

Stage One: Choose the Habitual Thought

The first step in the creation of a new habitual thought is to frame it in *toward language*; talk about what you want to start thinking instead of what you want to stop thinking. The easiest way to break an existing thinking habit is to replace it with a different (more empowering) way of thinking. A recent example of mine was to stop drinking wine during the week. If I had framed the habit in those terms, then I would have been reminding myself of the thing I habitually wanted at the very point when I most wanted it. I had to replace it with the habit of drinking my favorite tea. In toward language, my chosen habit was to drink tea in the evening, Monday to Thursday, because that was a healthier choice for me. However, that is a "doing habit" and is therefore less likely to stick—and would need more willpower to drive it. I therefore had to develop a new way of thinking that would support my new chosen behavior. I had to ground that new way of thinking deep within my psyche.

It's true that I needed to cut down on my wine consumption, because all the health advice told me to. However, changing a habit that I enjoyed was going to be tough if I was doing it simply because I felt I had been "told" to. I had to ground the roots of the new habit a little deeper. I therefore thought about what I wanted from the new habit. I wanted to feel more hydrated and have more energy each day. Honestly, I doubted that cutting out a glass or two of wine would make a radical difference. I therefore had to go even deeper to find the "hook" that would secure the new habit.

On the face of it, my wine drinking issue is a minor one, and that's the point of my using it as an example. Most of us don't get to change the world with one extraordinary step; rather, transforming our life by leading the relationship with ourselves means that we prioritize what we desire most out of life by making the right choices every single day. The first step, then, is to be really clear about what lights our fire: What do we most desire to be in life? My desires are to live a healthy and energized life, to be of service to others, to build strong and loving relationships and to be the best of which I am capable every day. I thought about the new habit in the context of how it would help me fulfill my desire to live a healthy and energized life, because the new habit allowed me to look after my liver better and the weekly change would translate into a significant improvement in my health over my lifetime. I developed the positive thought "I am loving my liver," and that served as a powerful mental anchor for me because it was linked to my desire to live healthily.

Only 8 percent of the resolutions we say we will implement every New Year are maintained. There are a number of reasons that the rate is so low; our resolutions are normally focused on what we will "do," they are often framed in negative language, and they are based on what we "need" or "want" rather than linked to what we "desire." Let me give you a couple of examples; you make a New Year's resolution to lose fifteen pounds because you know you "need" to lose weight. However, you put on the weight because of habits you currently have—eating chocolate after dinner or having a biscuit with your coffee. You like doing those things—that's at the level of "want." Replacing an existing "want" habit with a "need" habit is not going to cut it—need will not trump want. You'll be unable to maintain the willpower, and your old habits will prevail. Even if you lift the new habit to the "want" level—you want to lose fifteen pounds so that you can fit into your favorite dress or trousers for the party or wedding—it will give your current habit a run for its money, but you're still going to use up a lot of willpower to maintain the new action long enough to ritualize it. If you are able to link the new habit to what really lights you up inside and frame it as a positive way of thinking, then you reduce the amount of willpower you are going to spend to maintain it to a point where it becomes ritualized. If your desire is to be a great father or mother, then losing that extra weight will enable you to more easily chase your children around the garden or play football in the park with them. Your new habit could be "I'm a fit and healthy mom," accompanied by an inspiring mental image of what losing that weight will allow you to do more easily.

Saying that phrase and anchoring it to that inspiring image will mean that you are less reliant on pure willpower when you want to reach for that biscuit in the afternoon. Being clear about what really matters to us in life and who we believe we are capable of being is the inspirational hook upon which we can hang those apparently innocuous habits that, bit by bit, will transform our lives and enable us to become the best of which we are capable. Our desires will turbocharge our willpower so that, in no time, the new thought and action become effortlessly ritualized and part of who we are. However, we have to consciously coach ourselves so that we find the motivational "hook"—being our own coach is a key skill in leading the relationship with ourselves.

The first stage is, therefore, to consciously choose a positively stated thinking habit that is linked to what lights you up inside.

Stage Two: Be Aware of the Impulse Point

The "impulse point" is the trigger that will set off the old habitual routine. In the case of my wine drinking, my impulse point was that I would arrive home from work in the evening to my husband preparing our evening meal. I'd pour each of us a glass of wine and sit at the kitchen table to chat to him while he was cooking. It was the association of those events in the early evening that created the impulse for the old "routine."

The impulse point is when we are most vulnerable and need a high level of willpower to stick to our new habitual thinking and actions. The trouble is that the impulse point tends to be when our willpower is at a low ebb—in my case, at the end of the working day when I'm tired and my blood glucose levels are low. In the case of the chocoholic who wants a bar of chocolate with his afternoon cup of tea, his body most needs that burst of sugar when he's trying to resist it. In the case of the presenter who is riddled with self-doubt, she will find 101 things to do instead of sitting down to write the presentation.

The trick is to be aware of when the impulse point occurs and to plan for it. If it's that chocolate bar, then taking a healthy alternative and having it handy when the impulse arises is a practical solution. In the case of the procrastinator, promising herself that she only needs to prepare the outline of the presentation which will take her fifteen minutes—as long as the presentation isn't tomorrow—will help her get started.

Whereas early studies on habit forming indicated that every new routine—the new thinking habit that we're talking about—required a reward in order to be ritualized, that thinking has evolved in more recent studies. It is now understood that a sufficient "reward" for the new thinking or action is to focus on the *benefits* that the new habitual thinking *brings us*. We are evolutionarily hardwired to immediately remember negative events but not positive ones. That helped us survive an attack by a saber-toothed tiger millennia ago. If we want to create an attachment to the new habit—which will then help the ritualization process—then consciously focusing for at least twelve seconds on the positive outcomes that it generates will produce a positive, subconscious trigger when we next face the impulse point. When reflecting on my success at the end of a wine-free evening, I did so consciously, for twelve seconds or more, noticing how proud I felt of my new healthy habit and focusing on how I was cleansing my liver, day by day. I also took time to notice how great I felt each morning, to reinforce the positive reward.

The second stage is to be aware of, and plan for, the impulse point.

Stage Three: Repeat, and Repeat Again

> *"We are what we repeatedly do.*
> *Excellence then is not an act, but a habit."*
> **—Aristotle**

If we want the new habitual thinking to become part of the programming contained in our subconscious mind, then we need to work consciously on repeating it as the neurons start to wire together. Neurons associated with a certain activity or thought, function together and form a neural pathway. Through practice or repeated actions, the connections of these neural pathways become established and stronger. Therefore, with continuous training and practice, we are rewiring our neural pathways according to the habit we want to form. In a 2010 study to investigate the process of habit formation in everyday life, ninety-six volunteers chose an eating, drinking or behavior activity to carry out daily, in the same context—for example, after breakfast—for twelve weeks.[9] The study found that for the majority of participants, *automaticity*—the degree to which the activity becomes automated—increased steadily over the days of the study, thereby supporting the assumption that repeating a behavior in a consistent setting increases said automaticity. The findings of the study support the view that the early "repetitions" of a new way of thinking will have a significant impact on the ritualization of the habit. There is a point at which the habit cannot become any more "automatic" through repetition; it has essentially become part of your "programming." In turn, that means it has reached the point where the least possible willpower will be required to think the thought— "the plateau."

The average point at which the plateau was reached in the study was sixty-six days, with some volunteers reaching a plateau as early as eighteen days. The study also showed that a missed opportunity—an occasion when the action was not performed—did not materially affect the habit-forming process—so, if you fall off the horse, just get right back on it, because the "pathway through the forest" is still forming. When we are motivated by our desires to adopt a new habitual-thinking pattern, and we are therefore highly committed to it, the length of time it will take to become habituated in that new thinking pattern may well be at the lower end of the range identified by this study. So, three to five weeks of thinking your consciously chosen thought will be long enough to embed it as your new "default setting." This step requires you to work consciously and constantly on the new way of thinking—in the first three weeks in particular—to allow the neural pathway to form and for the thinking to evolve as your new habitual way of seeing yourself.

Anecdotally, my clients have consistently reported that the new way of thinking becomes part of their automatic response to external events within a fairly short period of time—normally within two to four weeks, and I've found that to be mirrored in my own experience.

The third stage is to repeat, repeat, repeat.

Stage Four: Engage Your Brain Power
In stage three, we saw that repetition enables the neural pathways to form to create the new habitual response. That's another way of saying that we are altering our subconsciously programmed response. The fourth stage is a powerful way of assisting the development of the new neural pathway. Let me return for a moment to the piano-playing experiment conducted by Harvard Medical School. A second group of volunteers was asked to merely "think" about practicing the piano exercise. They played the simple piece of music in their heads, holding their hands still, while imagining how they would move their fingers had they been physically playing the piece. They too did this exercise for two hours per day over five days. When the scientists compared the data from the two groups—those who actually played the piano and those who only imagined doing so—they saw that *mere thought* altered the physical structure and functions of the brain. The scans showed that the region of the motor cortex that controls the piano-playing fingers also expanded in the brains of volunteers who imagined playing the music, just as it had done in those who had actually played it.

If you have never tried visualization before now, I hope that news of the results of this study will encourage you to give it a go. It's particularly powerful in assisting the building up of cortical "real estate"—helping to strengthen that path through the forest, because the subconscious mind cannot distinguish between what is real and what is visualized with sufficient intensity.

Visualization can take the form of imagining oneself carrying out the new activity, or creating a negative or positive association to support the new habit or undermine the old habit. By way of example, when I was creating the new habit of drinking tea from Monday to Thursday, I wanted to build a negative association with wine so that I didn't have to rely entirely on my willpower at the end of a long day when my blood glucose levels were likely to be impaired at my peak impulse point. I did two things. Firstly, I created a visualization routine when I was able to sit undisturbed for a few moments; I closed my eyes and imagined a bottle of red wine. I tuned in to look at the glass bottle with the light reflecting off it, the gold and burgundy print of the label, the smell of the wine as it rose from the neck of the bottle, and imagined the glugging sound the wine would make as I poured it from the bottle, and the taste of it on my tongue. Just at that moment, I imagined a spider crawling out of the neck of the bottle, and a second and a third. I saw the hairs on the legs of the insects and heard the noise they made on the bottle as they came out of it. I imagined the smell of the wine turning sour and the sight of the dead, remaining spiders as I poured the wine from the bottle into the glass. I only had to do the visualization exercise twice to find that my strong desire for a glass of wine when my impulse point occurred had diminished radically! If your lip is curling right now, the same approach is likely to work for you too. I certainly succeeded in breaking the pleasant association I had with wine.

I could have chosen to use a visual image that built my pleasant association with tea. Instead, I made the making of tea a pleasant experience by involving several accoutrements such as tea leaves, china teapot, milk jug and so on. You may be concerned that using a technique such as negative association could have the effect of putting you off a specific item entirely, rather than just for a certain period. Interestingly, I found that I could continue to enjoy red wine when the normal "cue" did not arise, such as on a Saturday evening. The visualization technique did not impair my enjoyment of wine to any extent. I was just conscious that my impulse point arose when my willpower was normally impaired, and so I chose the more radical technique of creating a negative association and focused on it at the impulse point.

Visualization is also useful to enhance step three, the repetition step, because, in the form of "mental rehearsal," visualization has a similar effect in developing the neural pathways that enable the habit to become ritualized, as the practical completion of the new habit itself, just as in the Harvard piano study.

When I was learning to ride a motorbike, I used just such a technique. I had scheduled twelve riding lessons, and then my motorbike test, as part of a package. At the point when I had completed seven lessons, I became involved in a client project, which meant that I had to spend several weeks in southeast England. Because I was away from home, I wasn't able to participate in the lessons that I'd prebooked. In fact, because of my schedule, I would only be able to return home for the final lesson in the hour before the test and for the test itself. My instructor offered to reschedule the lessons and the test. I declined. I wanted to experiment with this technique of visualization that I'd heard so much about and to see if I could develop a positive mind-set about passing the test, as well as habituate those skills involved in riding a motorbike. I knew the test route and used that as the basis for my visualization, imagining the whole experience with each of my five senses, from starting up the bike engine to turning it off at the end of my virtual navigation of the test route. I really tuned in to what I would see, hear, feel, taste and smell had I actually been riding the bike around the route. I could feel the vibration of the engine as I turned the key in the ignition; I could smell the exhaust fumes, hear the change in the tone of the engine as I moved up and down the gears and taste the concentration in my mouth. I could see every detail of the test route as I "rode" along the familiar streets. Interestingly, I always remembered to turn off the indicator once I'd completed my left or right turn—something I had continually forgotten to do during my lessons!

When I turned up for my final lesson, my instructor looked a little queasy. I could see why; taking a test after only seven lessons—carried out four weeks earlier, and a final lesson just before the test—was a tall order for someone who'd never ridden a motorbike before sitting her initial 50cc test only four months before. However, I felt calm and confident, and as soon as I got on the motorbike, it felt comfortable and familiar. As I rode around the route with my instructor, I automatically did what was required, and felt at ease and peculiarly calm while doing it. I passed my test without difficulty. What I want to stress, though, is that the value of visualization lies in the brain changes that occur when the visualization is carried out with commitment, and the emotional changes that arise as a result of the increased association with a positive outcome. In the appendix, you will find a further explanation of the visualization process, as well as some suggested exercises to help you in leading the relationship with yourself by developing empowering thinking patterns.

The fourth stage is to engage your brain power.

Applying the four stages of habit forming requires us to be conscious and mindful until the new thinking pattern forms roots in our subconscious mind. "Mindfulness" represents a new way of "being" for most of us; testament to that are the repetitious thoughts that we think day after day. However, mindfulness is a habit worth cultivating and will be invaluable in helping you monitor your thinking so that you can ensure that the thoughts you have today are not entirely the same as those you had yesterday.

One of the most common habitual-thinking patterns that I have come across in my coaching practice is: "I'm not good enough." People can develop powerful coping mechanisms to hide this subconscious "truth," and may have excelled in life despite it, but the amount of effort and strain it takes to succeed while this mental program is running is extraordinary. Within a relatively short period of time and a commitment to the four-stage process, this disempowering thinking pattern can be overwritten with an empowering program. My clients have, without exception, been able to overwrite the old program with a new way of thinking about themselves and their potential, and have thereby removed the single greatest barrier to being the best of which they are capable. By choosing a new thought—such as "I am good enough just as I am" or "I can do anything I set my mind to" or "I have all I need to fulfill my potential" or any other phrase that fits with their desires—they achieve a shift which forms the foundation for building a new confidence. Simply overwriting that one program has changed the way they see themselves and enabled them to approach situations and interactions with a firm belief that they will succeed. By doing so, they are leading their thinking and not following old programming; they are leading the relationship with themselves. That is why developing *thinking* habits instead of *doing* habits will bring about profound progress in becoming your best self by supporting new actions and behavior that reflect who you believe you are. A new "action" habit is built on a foundation of sand if you haven't first worked on the underlying thinking that will undermine its success.

Just imagine what your life would look like if you took the lead in your thinking by ritualizing one empowering habit after another. By re-laying your mental landscape according to who you are now— your authentic self—you would gain clarity and confidence about your future. You would settle into your own skin, without trying to escape or change shape or hide behind a façade.

CHAPTER 3

LIVING A LIFE OF TRANSFORMATION BY TAKING THE LEAD IN THE RELATIONSHIP WITH YOURSELF

The Vision of Your Future:
True Wellness, Calm, Confidence and Energy

The Vision

In this chapter, I'd like to take you on a tour of a landscape: the dramatically changed landscape of your future once you choose to lead a relationship with yourself by developing empowering thinking habits. Let's imagine your old neural pathways as forming a map of your past thinking. The narrow contours of your former programming depicted steep peaks of anxiety, sharp falls in confidence and undulations in your self-esteem. By leading the relationship with yourself and developing empowering thinking, you have altered your neural pathways, broadened the contours and smoothed the passage through your everyday life. Healthy levels of positive stress have replaced the peaks of anxiety; a supportive inner voice has enabled you to develop confidence; and by stopping the perpetual concern about how the external world views you, you have created space for your authentic and empowered self to bud and grow. The strain of living every day through the ups and downs of your old thinking has been replaced with an easy knowing that you can change your perspective and, therefore, change the landscape.

Using That Vision as an Inspiration to Ritualize the Everyday Thinking That Will Get You There

There will be days when you are stressed and tired and find that you default to the familiarity of your old thinking. Those are the days when you might slip into the comfort of traveling down the spiral of "what's the point?" But that's just the shadow of the old contours, and those are the days when you need to be strong, take the lead in the relationship with yourself and pull yourself back into the new landscape. By developing the core habits that we spoke about in chapter 2, you will have created a solid foundation for making that transition back to leading the relationship with yourself. It will be like flicking from autopilot to turbocharge!

The Ideal Relationship—with Yourself

The life-changing happens on the inside. This is a wonderful truth, because you are in the driver's seat. You control what happens here— on the inside. By consciously self-coaching, you will have created a calm space inside yourself where you can think what you consciously choose to think, or you can let your mind rest while you enjoy the present moment. You can look out to the external world and notice what you see and experience, but whether you allow that experience to invade the tranquility of your internal world is your choice. You must choose sometimes to fully experience emotional pain: grief, sorrow, regret, anger and other charged emotions, because that is your way of working through an experience about which you care deeply. However, you will now feel those emotions deliberately, consciously, knowing that you are purposefully working through them to the other side, rather than avoiding them or wallowing in them. You now have perspective, which will allow you to compassionately watch your journey through the pain—not getting stuck permanently in the emotions themselves.

You are now consciously aware of your needs and boundaries and can communicate any anger or resentment to others articulately and proportionately. You know yourself transparently; you understand why you feel the way you do, and you love your warts and your roses. You understand that, in order to make others happy, *you* need to be happy and in balance; and lastly, you know that making yourself happy and keeping yourself in balance is your own responsibility.

The Transformed Life

The Effect of Ritualizing the Habit of Thought Awareness

As a person who now instinctively watches his or her thoughts like an objective observer, your "resting state" is to be calm and "unhooked." On the very rare occasions now when something or someone triggers your old thinking, it amuses you, because you recognize that this is the top of the "slippery slope," and you are able to nimbly sidestep it, returning to your resourceful repertoire. Others experience you as thoughtful and measured, and your increased personal presence has them focused more intently on what you have to share. Because you have developed the habit of watching your thinking, you no longer lose hours and days, replaying the same old mental tune as most people do. Your thinking is conscious and, therefore, responsive to the here and now. Today looks and feels different from yesterday because your thinking is a response to the present moment and to the new challenges that you have to face, rather than locked in rehearsing and rehashing yesterday's problems.

The Effect of Ritualizing the Habit of Listening to Your Compassionate Inner Voice

Your compassionate inner voice has become a soothing and supportive comforter, a champion in times of struggle. It's your cheerleader and your development coach. As a result of ritualizing the habit of listening to your compassionate inner voice, all self-criticism has melted away. Yes—you do make mistakes, but you now know that growth comes from failure only when we are able to learn objectively what went wrong and to plan constructively how to approach the same situation in the future. Your inner champion is able to hold that position of objective and constructive adviser. And from this new perspective, all the time that you used to spend wringing your hands and beating yourself up about things that you could not change seems like such a ridiculous waste of time. *If only everyone could learn how much more constructive this way of thinking is*, you muse. Then you remember—with an acknowledgment of the irony of it—how you first balked at the idea that changing how you speak to yourself could have such a dramatic impact on how you feel about yourself and, therefore, how you project yourself to others. You have a sense of inner confidence that you have never felt before—a knowing that whatever happens, you will be able to deal with it. With that knowledge comes a reassuring calm.

The Effect of Ritualizing the Habit of Mindfulness

By becoming conscious of the present moment, you now realize how much of your time you used to spend thinking about the past, ruminating on things you could not change or painting a picture of a desired future. And even now that you have developed the habit of bringing your attention back to the present moment, time and again, you are perpetually amazed at just how flighty the mind can be. Like a butterfly, the mind flits around, and try as you might to have it stay in a single moment, it takes off again toward the past or the future. In the moments when you are able to tame that butterfly, you feel calm, settled and happy. Presence, even in the toughest of times, is tolerable. Everything in the present moment is accompanied by the knowledge that soon it will pass. That means that you hungrily savor precious moments when they arise, before they melt away. In uncomfortable moments, you can sit with the pain, because you know that it too will pass, and a more tolerable experience will take its place.

The Effect of Ritualizing the Habit of Releasing the Past

Having cultivated this habit, you have released yourself from a dozen prisons of resentment and rumination. By listening intently to your inner critic, you have come to realize how much you have been holding against yourself—angry at the choices you made and ashamed of how you behaved in some key moments in your life. That intense self-loathing began to dissolve the minute you acknowledged that you had a choice to either let it go or to continue to allow it to infect the present and your future. The process of forgiving yourself has been slow and painful, but it has been worth it. It has enabled you to open your heart and feel the gentleness of release. That part of leading the relationship with yourself has perhaps been the hardest, because it has meant shattering the self-identity that you have been hiding from the world; and now the two parts of you—that which you project to the world and that which you have kept hidden—can merge to enable you to live life with less effort and a greater expectation of acceptance, beginning with your acceptance of yourself. From there, you have been able to change the script of how others have wronged you and robbed you of opportunities that could have been yours. That script has stolen from you so many more things than the initial wrongdoing, and you now realize that it is in your power to release those thoughts. You enjoy the lightness of letting any feelings of regret go, as they don't serve you. It's time to move on.

The Effect of Ritualizing the Habit of Creating Positive Expectations of Yourself

How limited were the old expectations of yourself! Your fear of failure, your belief that you had to be perfect to be lovable, your certainty that you were unworthy kept you small. Being invisible was the safest space to occupy. Now that you have rejected that old programming as absolutely, indubitably, unquestionably wrong, wrong, wrong, you can fly. You know without question that you are good enough exactly as you are. Hell, you're unstoppable as you are. You understand now that the only limits are those that you place on your imagination. You lead the relationship with yourself with gusto—pushing the walls away whenever you feel the oppression of any kind of limited thinking. You test new ideas, raising your own expectations of what life can bring you and what you can bring to life, from one level to the next. You've gone way beyond what you thought you were capable of, and the excitement of knowing that the best way to predict your future is to create it has you dreaming with desire.

The Effect of Ritualizing the Habit of Replacing Old Programming with New, Empowering Thought Patterns

You've learned to play with this habit. Anytime a contour from the old map seeps through to your current thinking, you see it for the redundant software that it is. You play with flipping it on its back and replacing it with the opposite belief, and you get to work, proving that the selected belief is an accurate hallmark of who you now are.

Focus on What Is Truly Important to You

"Things which matter most must never be
at the mercy of things which matter least."
— **Johann Wolfgang von Goethe**

When all the mental noise dies down—as it will when you are leading a relationship with yourself—you will have space to focus on what is truly important to you. There are only two directions in life: toward love or toward fear. Much of our disempowering programming arose from a need to protect ourselves or cope with difficult situations. Those thinking patterns tended to be about defending ourselves and kept us stuck in fearful thinking. When we have developed the habit of leading a relationship with ourselves, much of the fearful thinking is replaced with more empowering thinking patterns. But in order to consciously focus on what is truly important to us, it can be helpful to keep in mind the two directions of fear and love and to test every decision against that spectrum. A seesaw will remain steady when weights of an equal measure are placed on either side, and the fulcrum is set right at the center. Move the fulcrum, and a heavier weight will need to be placed at the shorter end of the plank to keep the seesaw balanced. If we were to view one end of the seesaw as what we love, and the other as what we fear, then placing all our focus (the weight) on what we fear means that we have to locate our energy (the fulcrum) on holding up those fears. The same principle applies to focusing our energy on what we love— what is truly important to us. We make hundreds of decisions every day—some large, many small. Developing the habit of asking yourself, in respect to both large and small decisions, "Will saying yes to this take me in the direction of what I love, or in the direction of what I fear?" will keep your focus on what is truly important to you. A life well lived is made up of a series of decisions like this, and it's what we do every day that leads to a future relationship with ourselves that is filled either with self-loathing or with self-love.

Your Vision of Wellness

Whatever "wellness" means to you, you are able to make decisions about how you treat your body and your mind every day. Those daily decisions take you closer either to how you love to feel or how you loathe to feel. What is your vision of wellness? Is it being physically fit and flexible; feeling calm and present; nourishing your body with great food? The first step is to have a vision of what is important to you in terms of your physical and mental wellness. The next step, of course, is to take action. As we know from the four-step habit-forming process, that action begins with positively stating the habit from a perspective of what you most desire rather than simply what you want or need. So, in engaging with your vision of wellness, what do you most desire for yourself in six months, twelve months, over a lifetime? This is not about a short-term diet, it's about building wellness habits that align entirely with how you want to live your life and that take you in the direction of what you love rather than what you fear. Short-term diets often come from a place of being self-critical—hating what we see in the mirror. Fitness regimes can be prompted by the same mind-set. Food can be used to assuage fear or find comfort. These motivators have the fulcrum supporting the fear or loathing and won't be able to sustain the wellness habits. Be gentle with yourself and understand that a small wellness habit is a start, and it will support the gradual adoption of more significant habits. Wellness habits can only be effortlessly sustained when you have established your internal "champion"—your compassionate inner voice. I was asked recently, "What happens when we revert to unhealthy behaviors because we're going through a tough time?" My answer: be gentle with yourself. If we berate ourselves for drinking too much alcohol or eating the wrong food, we have flipped back into the habit of our inner voice being our inner vice. Sometimes we need to feel pain and fall off the wagon as a way of stabilizing ourselves. By gently coaching ourselves to focus on one small wellness habit while understanding that time will take care of the rest, we can move the fulcrum to the constructive end of the seesaw.

Your Vision for How You Spend Your Time

Now that you have clarity about what is truly important to you in life, you are determined to spend your time wisely so that you can cultivate those important components, whatever they may be. You understand fully that you are able to exercise a conscious choice in about how to spend every moment of every day. You've heard yourself make all the excuses about how the barrage of emails you receive every day is what drives your priorities, but now you see that that was just an excuse for failing to take responsibility for prioritizing what was important to you. Now that you are leading the relationship with yourself, you intently focus on every moment so that you are engaging in any task with your full attention, and know that this is the most vital thing to be doing right now. You relish the new habit of playing with your son before bedtime rather than slumping together in front of the television. You love eating together as a family rather than eating on the run. You are much more conscious of scheduling meaningful family or together time on the weekend, rather than "taking it as it comes." You appreciate that you are "making" your children's memories, and want to spend time adding color and texture to those memories, as well as helping them develop healthy thinking habits—like enjoying the present moment.

Your Vision for How You Spend Your Energy

Energy is a precious resource. You used to squander it daily by thinking about things you could not change, worrying about what other people thought of you, stressing over what might or might not happen. Now you appreciate that there is a much more constructive route to getting value for your worry. If you are annoyed about how someone spoke to you during the meeting, you now use your energy to work out what you are going to do to address that with that person. Rather than worry about the cost of the car repairs, you take steps to find out the facts and your options. Rather than being stressed about the interview, you now focus on what more you can do to prepare and what visualization techniques you can use to assist with overwriting that old programming.

You treat your energy as a precious resource. Leading the relationship with yourself means that you spend your energy mindfully and consciously, and you make sure to get "bang" for your energy buck.

How to Maintain Your Motivation

Leading a relationship with yourself means that you have developed the skill of self-motivation. Imagine it: you can get anything done just by putting your mind to it. Like any skill, there are some steps to master. Scott Geller, a professor at Virginia Tech and director of the Center for Applied Behavior Systems in the Department of Psychology, sets out four aspects that require being present in order to maintain our motivation to achieve change. Those are:

1. We believe that we can make the change, and that it will work.
2. We believe that the consequences are worth the effort.
3. We have a choice about whether to make the change or not.
4. We have support in making the change.

Take step one: by leading the relationship with yourself, you have developed the habit of selecting empowering thinking. Of course you believe you can make the change and that you can make it work!

Turning to step two, you had a vision of the life of transformation you could live if you ritualized core habits, and that's what kept you motivated when the going got tough. You will continue to create inspiring visions of the next step in this adventure, and they will motivate you to keep thinking that you can do whatever you set your mind to.

The key issue about the third step is that you continue to develop habits that take you in the direction of what you love and desire, that will make the choice to think in the new way and the challenge of overcoming the impulse point less effortful.

The fourth step is, that by leading a relationship with yourself, you are able to coach and cajole yourself and have a supportive, compassionate inner voice. It's also helpful to find a like-minded friend or supportive family member to give you encouragement and believe in you.

Whenever you feel your motivation lagging, it's worth revisiting this little checklist to diagnose the cause, fix the problem and get back on the wagon. It's worth the (diminishing) effort required to make the new habit stick—I promise!

Your Internal Barometer

> *"You will become way less concerned with what*
> *other people think of you when you realize how seldom they do."*
> —**David Foster Wallace**, *Infinite Jest*

A barometer is used to measure atmospheric pressure. Its usefulness comes from being a device by which we can measure something that we cannot precisely measure by using our own judgment. When I ask clients whether they agree with the statement "What others think of me is more important than what I think of myself," many do agree. Most of us have been brought up to look outward for approval and for an indication of how we are doing. The set up within our education system tends to cause us to measure ourselves against others. However, unlike barometers, whether we are being and doing the best of which we are capable is something that we *can* measure by using our own judgment.

If we use the opinion of others as the barometer, then the reading will be faulty. Their opinion of us will normally be corrupted by how they see themselves and how we measure up in comparison with that perspective. Leading a relationship with yourself means trusting your own judgment about whether you are being the best of which you are capable. Sure, we can ask the people who truly want the best for us, for their view of things, but that is an ingredient to be weighed into the mix rather than the entire recipe. As we cultivate the habit of "checking in" rather than "checking out," we will increase our trust in our own judgment—after all, we are no longer the pinball in the machine!

CHAPTER 4

LEADING THE RELATIONSHIP TO FRUITION

Aligning Yourself with Your Inner Purpose

"He who has a why to live can bear almost any how."
—Friedrich Nietzsche

 purpose enables us to find meaning in the activities and experiences of our lives—it's finding the "why" in what we are doing or experiencing, or planning to achieve.

Making Your Unique Contribution to the World

"The purpose of life is a life of purpose."
—Robert Byrne

53

Having a purpose in life is good for your health. A study published in 2012 had volunteers undergo cognitive and neurological testing once a year for ten years.[10] Each person was asked to clearly define his or her purpose in life. After each participant's death, brain autopsies were performed on them. The researchers found that people who did not have a clear purpose in life had significantly faster rates of mental decline. This study also linked not having a purpose in life to decreased longevity and a higher risk of Alzheimer's disease.

The essence of leading a relationship with yourself is really getting to know who you authentically are, behind the veil of programming and conditioning. Unless you know who you authentically are, it's difficult to identify what gives your life meaning and, therefore, what your purpose in life is. You are the only person on this planet with your blend of strengths, values, interests and motivators. You may feel that you have been wasting your energy "getting by" and doing what needs to be done to pay the mortgage and put food on the table. You may currently invest your energy every day in doing things that you don't really believe in and maintaining relationships that are vital to you staying "safe" in an environment that does not give you joy. You will already have become restless in that environment if you have begun to develop the habit of leading a relationship with yourself. Finding work and an environment that is aligned to your purpose will transform your morning routine from repeatedly hitting the "Snooze" button to leaping out of bed, full of anticipation for a day filled with challenges that you know are worthwhile—and you will still be able to pay the mortgage and put food on the table. Doing meaningful work energizes and engages your creative thinking and makes you much more fun to be around. Rather than draining your energy, work will invigorate you and deliver you home to your family at the end of each day, with enough energy to enjoy the people who matter in your life. Striving to find your purpose in life is ultimately the desired destination of those who choose to lead the relationship with themselves.

Do You Value Yourself Enough to Want to Identify Your Purpose?
We are constantly letting other people know how to treat us by the way we treat ourselves. In the past, you may have spent a lot of energy hiding who you believed you really were from the world, and projecting the image that you wanted the world to see. Now we know that, until we accept ourselves as we authentically are and lead our relationship with ourselves by developing empowering habits, we will not be in a position to fulfill our potential. Until we accept ourselves as we are, our identity will be dependent entirely on the good opinion of others.

At this point, your inner critic may resurface from the depths of those faded contours—it will block your ability to fulfill your potential if you allow it to. That inner critic will ask, "Who are you to consider yourself grand enough to have a purpose?" It may make snide comments as you work through the exercises in this section. You now know that you can engage conscious choice in deciding whether to listen to your inner critic or recognize it as a legacy from your past that does not fit with who you now are. If you want to live a life of meaning, then learning to value yourself and the contribution that you can make to the world is a habit you must cultivate.

Each of us is unique. We each have a contribution to make which could impact the world in a way quite unlike the contribution made by another. Our challenge is to identify those components that make us unique and to deploy them to their best effect. However, this also requires us to step out of the framework set around us by others and to embrace the challenge of working out the puzzle of who we truly are and how to unlock the potential within us. To solve that puzzle, we need to explore what our values are, what naturally piques our interest and create an inventory of our strengths.

Solving the Purpose Puzzle

Identify Your Values

Our values are our principles or standards of behavior; our judgment of what is important in life. Our values guide our personal choices and our perception of the worth of others. We usually apply our values, subconsciously, when making judgments about things and people, and we tend to subconsciously respect someone who shares our values.

On an individual level, it is vital to understand what our core values are. In doing so, we can use them as a "check list" against which we measure the pros and cons of every important decision we need to make in our lives. Often, people seeking a more meaningful direction in life are clear about what they don't want and less clear about what they do want to do in the future. Below, I've set out a list of values—it isn't an exhaustive list, so please feel free to choose any that do not appear on the list. The list is simply here to help get you started. Please choose the eight values from the list that you identify as being most important to you. By that, I mean those values that would guide your personal choices or that would influence your perception of another person if they displayed or failed to display those values.

Love	Integrity	Flexibility
Security	Success	Humor
Health	Freedom	Kindness
Happiness	Compassion	Independence
Money	Trust	Excitement
Adventure	Equality	Justice
Travel	Respect	Friendship
Honesty	Achievement	Fitness
Loyalty	Acceptance	Making a difference
Family	Fun	Contribution
Power		

Once you have listed the eight values that are most important to you, I'd like you to strike out the three values that least resonate with you from that list. It's a struggle, I know, but please go ahead and do it. You now have your five "core values." Please check your list and make sure it reflects what is most important to you in life—these are your core principles.

What Is the Relevance of Your Values to the Decisions You Make?
Are there any key decisions that you need or want to make at the moment? Do you crave a change of career or want to move jobs within your existing career? If your current role is failing to reflect your values, then think about how any prospective role might meet them more closely. When I was thinking about resigning my role as partner, I wanted to be clear about what my core values were. I went through the process outlined above and arrived at my (then) core values. They were: freedom, flexibility, love, contribution and adventure. I was in a well-remunerated role where I worked long hours and helped my clients to manage risk and save money. The only value of mine that was being met was "contribution," in the sense that I did feel that I made a difference to the working lives of my team members, through my style of leadership, and to the experience of my clients, when they faced a stressful situation, by the way in which I related to them. Even so, that single value was not being fulfilled as much as I would have liked; I did not feel as if I was making any lasting difference but simply helping clients overcome their current and most pressing problems. I had no flexibility or freedom, as I worked long hours in a fairly regimented environment. I faced a challenge that many of us face: I knew my current environment wasn't fulfilling my values, but I wasn't clear about what my purpose or unique contribution might be. I still had some work to do on that front—I needed to identify what my natural strengths were and where my interests lay.

Identify Your Strengths

We all have a unique combination of strengths or talents. They are aspects of us that are often innate but can also be learned. They can be personality traits, characteristics or more value-based expressions of who we are. The purpose of this section is for you to identify your natural strengths.

When I coach on this aspect of the purpose exercise, I have noticed that clients often find it difficult to articulate their natural strengths. Interestingly, modesty appears to be the most significant barrier. To overcome that, I ask them to imagine that I am having a conversation with a friend or relative who knows them very well and is aware of how they perform at work, how they behave in key relationships and the strengths that they have seen them deploy during significant challenges and achievements in their life. I ask them to tell me what that friend or relative might say are their five core strengths. Imagine that I have asked you to carry out that exercise. What might that person tell me about your strengths? Once you're ready, please list your five core strengths.

I recommend to you the VIA (Values in Action) Survey of Character Strengths, which is a lengthy questionnaire prepared by the VIA Institute under the direction of Christopher Peterson and Martin Seligman. The questionnaire will take approximately twenty-five minutes to complete and will rank your strengths from top to bottom, and will also give you further insight in to your values. The questionnaire can be found at www.authentichappiness.org.

By now, you should be starting to see some themes emerging from a comparison of your strengths and your values. When you look at those themes, they should resonate deeply with you as a true reflection of who you authentically are. If they don't, please revisit the exercises, and spend a little more time reflecting on what is really important to you in life—your code of honor—and also those strengths you've demonstrated when you've been at your very best.

What Are You Naturally Interested In?

Being interested is the feeling we get when our attention is particularly engaged by something. Being conscious of what naturally piques our interest is a very useful clue to our purpose. For example, I have always been interested in how people relate to one another, even as a child. I can talk for hours with others about how they can best make their relationships work effectively and fulfill their potential; I'm fascinated by what makes people tick. To find our natural interests, a great place to start is looking to those *activities* that naturally interest us, when time just seems to disappear when we are engaged in them. In a work context, it is useful to reflect on those occasions when your levels of engagement have been at their highest. It may be when you have been training others, managing a project, facilitating a discussion, solving a problem, designing a solution or process or creating a physical object. Our hobbies can also be a clue to our interests, as well as subjects that we can speak passionately about.

What Are Your "Repellent Elements"?

There are factors most often in our work environment that can inspire us, and others that repel us. A good mechanism for checking that you've accurately identified what interests you naturally, is to think of a work environment that you've found challenging and to focus in on the aspects that repelled you about the environment. Those may be the corporate structure, the politics, the bullying culture, lack of flexibility, feeling de-individualized and so on. We struggle in environments where our needs are not being met, and we can feel stifled, frustrated or bored. In those situations, our tendency is to revert to stress behaviors rather than to display our core strengths. Reflect for a moment on a time when you have been in an environment that made you feel unhappy or dissatisfied; what needs did you have that were not being met? What was it about that environment that didn't work for you? The answer to the first question should resonate with the interests that you have listed—and may be a reminder of one you've missed from the list. The answer to the second question will remind you of the elements of an environment that repel you.

Finding the "Why"

So far, we have been focusing on the "what," in terms of what a role and environment would have to offer in order for you to find meaning in the work that you do there. That role and environment would have to fit with your key values and enable you to demonstrate your strengths and play to your interests. The next question is: Why would you want to do the job? I know it sounds like we've already answered that question—it fits with your values, strengths and interests, and that's why you'd like to do the job. However, sometimes there is still a nagging doubt that you "should" be doing something else. The "should" prompt often arises from external pressures or perceived expectations.

Your Intrinsic Motivators

> *"Don't ask what the world needs—ask what makes you come alive and then go and do that. Because what the world needs is people who have come alive."*
> —**Howard Martin**

Intrinsic motivation is focusing on your own internal satisfaction or fulfillment—it's doing those things that "make you come alive" without the need for external reward or recognition. We've already talked about making sure that every decision you make, or thinking pattern you adopt, takes you toward the things that you love, and that's essentially what intrinsic motivation is about. Extrinsic motivation, on the other hand, is a drive to action that arises from external influences such as what others think of you, societal pressures and cultural expectations that may bear upon you. I encountered quite a bit of that when I resigned from my partner role. While I was clear about the fact that I was moving solidly in the direction of things that I loved to do, well-meaning friends, clients, colleagues and family members were keen to get me to focus on the other end of the seesaw: Did I realize what security I was giving up? Did I even have a job to go to? What about how hard I had worked to get to where I was? Let me be clear—it takes courage to follow a path that allows you to make a meaningful contribution, realizing it is scattered with people on the roadside who took the first step but then backed out. It's only when you have developed the empowering habits that enable you to lead in a relationship with yourself that you can take this step with certainty. All the work that you have been doing to lead your relationship has essentially been about clearing away all the programming debris, gaining clarity about who you are and what is important to you, so that you can walk confidently in the direction of the life you were destined to live.

Without clearing away the debris and gaining clarity, we remain stuck in focusing outside of ourselves for approval, belonging and meaning. In his book *Why We Do What We Do*, Edward L. Deci reports on findings made by researchers during a study that focused on three extrinsic aspirations, namely, money, fame, and beauty, and on three intrinsic aspirations, namely, meaningful relationships, personal growth and community contributions. The findings of the study were that those who had an unusually strong aspiration for material success were more likely to display narcissistic behavior, anxiety, depression and poorer social functioning as rated by a trained clinical psychologist, whereas strong aspirations for any of the intrinsic goals were positively associated with well-being. People who strongly desired to contribute to their community, for example, had more vitality and higher self-esteem. I believe that those who are driven by intrinsic desires are simply being authentic and are consciously leading the relationship with themselves in the direction of meaning.

One of my coaching clients described how the process worked for him, as follows.

> For me, this process took something that was barely perceptible, yet a source of discomfort, and shone a light on it. Perhaps most of us carry around baggage of this kind, and perhaps it infrequently causes enough discomfort for us to consciously decide to do something about it. When it does, and the light is on it, your first reaction is to want to get away from it, but with such a nebulous concept, it is actually quite impossible to do so. Understanding friends and family will try to offer you advice ranging from running away to join the circus to knuckling down to work and being thankful for what you have, but the process showed me that I had to run *toward* something in order to be relieved of the discomfort—even if that meant running toward the high wire. Chances are that you are not as far away from the right way of life for you as you might imagine. It may be that the solution is also hidden in plain sight, and once you have a handle on your values, it becomes a question of gently steering your ship in that direction and hopefully not having to jettison much of its contents. Overcoming the inclination to dismiss your discomfort as self-indulgence is the very first step—to get anywhere with this, you must feel entitled to live a fulfilling life, composed by your own inner being and not by the cultural pressures that surround us.

Making Your Current Work Meaningful
While You Find Your Work of Purpose

When you are clear about your values, you become clear about why an environment appeals to you or why you struggle with it. That understanding, of itself, can make a challenging situation more tolerable. Once you are explicit about your strengths, you can look for more opportunities to display those strengths within your current environment. Becoming clear about what your interests are enables you to focus on areas of interest in your present role. Finally, knowing what your intrinsic motivators are—what gives you meaning—enables you to focus on the opportunities in your present role that align with those desires. For example, someone who works in a call center, selling cable service plans, and who is motivated by building strong relationships could see every call as an opportunity to make his meaningful contribution. A good friend of mine took exactly that approach when working in a very pressured environment. She decided that she would connect with every person she spoke to so that she could make her meaningful contribution while working in an environment in which she'd have preferred not to be working. It not only dramatically increased her "joy factor" at work, but she noticed that those around her were mirroring her approach when taking calls from customers too. The truth is that we have an opportunity in every moment of every day to be who we authentically are, and to make our contribution to the world; we don't need to wait for the ideal environment. And actively looking for those opportunities will give you "interim joy"—while you are waiting for your ideal opportunity to show up.

Creating Your Purpose Action Plan

Studies have shown that fewer than 3 percent of us write down our goals. As John Wooden would say, "If you fail to plan, you plan to fail." Goals and actions are a very effective way of focusing your energy on the things that will move you in the direction you want to head. When we set a goal from a position of being clear about *why* it will give our life meaning, and how it will fulfill our strengths, values and interests, we require almost no willpower to achieve it. A clearly defined and motivating goal also engages our conscious thinking about what changes need to take place in order to achieve the goal.

> *"You can't build a reputation on what you're going to do. It's simple, fantasize, rehearse and then go out into the world and* do it!*"*
> —**Henry Ford**

What I've found in coaching people through the move to finding a role or environment in which they can make their meaningful contribution, is that it is rarely achieved in a single step. Often, that is because there are challenges relating to financial commitments, qualifications or experience. With financial challenges, it's often useful to do an inventory of your expenses so as to be clear about the minimum amount of money that you need to live on. Being honest about all the obstacles on the road ahead, and mapping them out clearly will be helpful in devising solutions to overcoming them. Here's a health warning: every client I have coached through this process (without exception) has had a "gulp" moment when setting out their financial commitments to determine how much money needs to keep coming in to live their life—even a less luxurious version of it. Stay with it. It may simply mean building in a couple of extra steps to your purposeful life. The most important step of all is to use the four-step habit-forming process to embed thinking that will support your desired direction.

Staying on the Path toward Passion

Once you've done the exercises set out earlier in the chapter, and the shape of your dream life starts to evolve, you will feel your passion ignite. Hold on to that feeling. Cherish it and cultivate it. Leading the relationship with yourself means that you will do all you can to keep the dream from being extinguished by the icy waters of everyday life. All the things you learned in chapter 1 will enable you to understand that self-doubt may well arise—but that's just old programming that is being triggered by the unfamiliar dream of a passionate life. The skills that we spoke about in chapter 2 will enable you to overwrite that programming with specifically tailored thinking that will catapult you toward your new plan. Chapter 3 will be your touchpoint—your inspirational vision for who you are becoming by leading a relationship with yourself. But just in case you are in need of additional "charge," let's look at some confidence-building techniques that will help you maintain your connection to your dreams.

Developing Confidence

Confidence is believing in yourself and your own ability to shape outcomes. If you lack confidence, you won't try, and your failure becomes a self-fulfilling prophecy. If you have confidence, your optimism about the outcome makes it far more likely that you will succeed. Having a clear set of goals, and habitual thinking that supports them, will be like rocket fuel to your confidence levels. But it also helps to be aware of a couple of tips that can supercharge your confidence when you most need it. Confidence is an emotion that you can create through your thinking, just as you can diminish confidence through your thinking or imagination. The exercise I am about to show you enables you, firstly, to generate the feelings of confidence, and then to set an "anchor" which will allow you to access those confident feelings when you want to. In chapter 2, we looked at the development of neural pathways in the brain, which ultimately create a new habitual-thinking pattern. We are going to apply those same principles during this exercise.

Associate the Achievement of Your Life of Purpose with a Feeling of Confidence

1. Sit down in a place where you won't be disturbed.
2. Relax by taking five deep breaths.
3. Think back to a time or times in your life when you felt confident. Relive them as if they were happening now, by seeing what you saw, hearing what you heard, feeling what you felt and tasting and smelling the environment you were in. Visualizing the memory with this degree of intensity helps develop the neural pathway. Remember, the Harvard piano experiment scientifically recorded the physical changes in the motor cortex that the visualization process can generate. Make the experience as intense as you can and concentrate on the feeling of confidence that swells up inside you.
4. Open your eyes and enjoy the feeling of confidence that remains, knowing that you can generate it whenever you want to.

Creating an Anchor or Trigger for Confident Feelings

Triggers are like icons on your computer screen—they are shortcuts to lengthy programs. Like Pavlov with his dog, you can create a mechanism that acts as a shortcut to achieving an emotional state. It's called a "neural trigger."

To carry out this exercise, repeat steps 1 through 3 in the preceding exercise. While visualizing the events and concentrating on the feeling of confidence, press your forefinger and thumb together, creating a degree of pressure. Focus on the pressure and the confidence simultaneously, aware that you are associating one with the other.

Repeat this exercise so that the neural pathway, associating the trigger of your thumb and forefinger with the feeling of confidence, becomes stronger and stronger. The more your repeat the exercise, the more established the pathway will become.

Now—confidently march in the direction of your purposeful life!

THE FIRST THIRTY DAYS OF LEADING A RELATIONSHIP WITH YOURSELF

I want you to experience the transformational effects of leading a relationship with yourself by developing empowering thinking habits, and so I've set out a couple of exercises that you can focus on during the next thirty days. I've chosen that period of time because it's long enough to enable you to ritualize these habits and to experience the significant difference that the new way of thinking will have in many of areas of your life. Invariably, my clients are astonished at how quickly and effectively the changes in their outlook occur, and then can't believe that they used to think in the old ways!

The Devil's Advocate Exercise

Let me introduce you to your "internal" coach: the devil's advocate. Despite his title, he has your best interests at heart. He simply wants to test the quality of your current thinking to see if a more helpful or constructive way of thinking can be found.

You can wheel out your devil's advocate ("DA" as we will affectionately call him) whenever you stumble across thinking that is keeping you stuck, either emotionally or creatively. That will tend to occur when you are dealing with expectations about what you can achieve, how you will perform, or when ruminating over past events or with tendencies to be negative or pessimistic about a particular subject. We'll call this "stuck thinking."

When you become aware of stuck thinking, take out a notepad and pen and imagine that your DA is asking you the following series of questions, then write down your answers to them.

1. What is the stuck thinking? (Write down the thought so that you can see it clearly.)
2. How is this thought hindering you in this situation? (Set out clearly how this thought is holding you back.)
3. How is this thought helping you in this situation? (Set out clearly any assistance that thinking in this way is giving you.)
4. How much, on a scale of 1 to10 (10 being the highest) do you want to change the way in which you are thinking about this situation? (If your score is less than 5, write out why. This would only normally occur if the stuck thinking is helping more than it is hindering, in which case reflect on why you have labeled it as "stuck thinking.")
5. What new thought or way of thinking would be more helpful? (Write down the thought or way of thinking that would be more helpful, using toward/positive language).
6. When you see the thought written down, how does it make you feel, and how closely do you identify with it? (This question is directed at whether you believe you can make the change and

whether it will work. See How to Maintain Your Motivation, in chapter 3.)

7. If you feel negative about or unidentified with the new thought, can you select a different thought with which you do feel identified?

This section of questions completes the first step of the habit-forming process.

8. When might you feel the impulse to revert to the old way of thinking? (Write down the impulse points or environment likely to occur.)

9. How can you plan to overcome the impulse to revert to the old way of thinking? (Write down the strategies to overcome the impulse.)

This section of questions completes the second step of the habit-forming process.

10. In what other situations does the stuck thinking impact negatively on your ability to be the best of which you are capable? (Write down any other current situations where the stuck thinking may have an adverse impact—the more examples you can come up with, the better.)

11. What can you do to maximize the opportunities for repeatedly applying this new way of thinking to the current situation and the other situations that you have identified? (This way of thinking becomes your new "mantra," and if you can repeat it frequently, you will be able to ritualize it more quickly.)

This section of questions completes the third step of the habit-forming process.

12. What would success look like if you lived your life on the basis that this new way of thinking was absolutely true? (Write down the ways in which your life might be affected by this new way of thinking.)

13. Are the positive consequences of making the change worth the effort? (This refers to step two in the How to Maintain Your Motivation section, in chapter 3.)

14. Is there any mental rehearsal or visualization technique that you could use to support your appetite to make the change and help with the development of the neural pathways? (In answering this question, it may help to look at the visualization exercises in the appendix.)

15. What other support might you be able to get in order to help habituate yourself to this new way of thinking? (This refers to step four in the motivation section in chapter 3. Please think about anyone who could act as a coach or mentor to give you feedback on what they notice as a result of this change in thinking.)

This section of questions completes the fourth step of the habit-forming process.

I recommend that you keep a journal detailing the changes you notice over the thirty day period after you have completed the DA exercise, because you will be able to track the point at which the new thinking becomes less effortful, and that will give you an idea of how quickly you are able to ritualize new thinking, as it is different for everyone. It does, however, become faster and easier the more you do it.

The Champion Exercise

I'd like you to think about someone in your life right now who cares deeply about you, is incredibly supportive and would argue your corner if anyone unjustifiably criticized you. Let's call that person your champion. I'm asking you to do this because we often use our inner critic to unjustifiably criticize ourselves, and that voice needs a counterbalance. That counterbalance is your champion.

Imagine that your champion has now taken up residence in your head and, somewhat alarmingly, can hear every thought you think.

Whenever your inner critic goes on a rampage, I'd like you to hear that thinking as if through the ears of your champion. How might those criticisms sound to him or her? Imagine what your champion would say in your defense to the inner critic, and listen carefully to the tone of their voices as they talk about you. Do not defend the position of criticism adopted by the inner critic. Just listen to what is said in your defense.

Reflect on what has been said by your champion about you and compare it what the inner critic has said. Which voice is most helpful in your growth and your drive to become the best of which you are capable? Assuming you agree that the compassionate voice gives you greater room for growth, then invite your champion (you can use your own title or description) to reside in your head permanently and kick the inner critic out, throwing his or her suitcase out too. The inner critic may come knocking at a later date. If it does, just smile and ignore it, turning the volume up on your compassionate inner voice.

Again, I recommend keeping a journal just to consciously notice how frequently the inner critic chatters on, and how it feels to be compassionate with yourself more frequently.

PART TWO

LEADING THE RELATIONSHIP WITH OTHERS

CHAPTER 5

IT'S TIME TO LOOK AT YOUR RELATIONSHIPS WITH OTHERS

If They'd Just Change, Then Everything Would Be Fine!

Relationships Are Complicated

Relationships with others are complicated. At least that's what most of us like to think. Relationships are our greatest source of happiness and can be our greatest cause of distress. They make our hearts soar and can make our hearts break. We often behave like passive passengers on a road trip in our relationship with another—complaining to the driver when the bumps in the road get too uncomfortable, when he or she drives to fast or too slow, or runs a red light. We follow the direction the other wants to take, and then complain about the destination.

We often fail to articulate what we need, and then mutter bitterly when our friends or mate can't read our mind and don't give us precisely what we want. We fail to lead the relationship with others because we have been failing to consciously lead the relationship with ourselves. Once you take internal responsibility for knowing who you authentically are, and creating a mental landscape that makes life navigable, and even joyful, then you come to realize that you also have the power—and the responsibility—to lead every relationship in your life to the best dynamic of which it is capable.

Looking Outward Rather Than Inward

Do you look "outward" in relationships with others—at what the other people are doing, saying and not saying? It's so simple from your perspective—why don't they just do this or that? Then everything would be fine. Like a dance, with them leading, and you following, you wait for them to change direction, but they appear oblivious to the shift in tempo. That's because there *hasn't* been a shift in tempo. For that to happen, *you* need to do something different. Passively waiting for others to change means that you keep doing the same things, behaving in the same ways, and yet you expect something different to happen. Albert Einstein would say that approach is insane. You may well have yelled, screamed or sulked about requests for change—in a way that, to you, seemed clear and articulate. But if your requests are charged with emotion and spoken from an unchanged mind-set, then they just won't be heard. It's as if you are waiting for permission to adapt how you behave in the relationship. The trouble is—the other person might be thinking exactly the same thing! It's a Wild West relationship standoff. With two "followers," and no one taking the lead, the relationship is going to keep going in the same direction until it crashes, as eventually it will.

Behavior Breeds Behavior

"Behavior breeds behavior" is a well-worn phrase because it's true. Behavior in one person will trigger the behavioral response in others—unless the "others" are in the habit of leading the relationship with themselves, that is. There are a host of things going on in an interaction, psychologically speaking. First of all, our focus—what we notice others—is determined by our perceptions of them. Secondly, their focus—what they notice about what we say and do—is determined by their perceptions of us. Those perceptions may have been developed over years, months, days or minutes. They may be shored up by lots of "evidence"—also "filtered in" through those perceptions—or an impression in the process of being formed. How we behave is determined by how effectively we lead the relationship with ourselves. If we haven't done much of the work in part 1 of this book, then we are at the mercy of our programming, are likely to react subconsciously to triggers, and we will be unable to *lead* this relationship to a healthier dynamic. We will have a "split identity"—one that we want to project in the relationship, and the self-identity that we would prefer to keep hidden. We are less likely to be stable in the relationship too—in the sense that we will react more instinctively to the "push and pull" than if we had developed the deep roots that come from leading the relationship with oneself.

If You Don't Value Yourself, Why Should They?

Relationships reflect the extent to which people engaged in them value themselves and one another. We are constantly showing others how we "deserve" to be treated by how we treat ourselves. If you don't value yourself, you will show that lack of regard in a million different ways. Your message to the world comes from how you meet it—either head-on or with your back turned, apologetic for who you are. If you enter a relationship of any kind with a need for it to complete you or support you in any way, then it's off-kilter from the start. That's not to say that you cannot turn to your friends, family or mate and ask for help and support—of course you must—from time to time. But if a permanent feature of that relationship is your "neediness," then it just won't be healthy. As Roberta M. Gilbert, MD put it, "The best relationships seem to enhance rather than hinder the individuality of both people. . . . If relationships are used in an attempt to complete the self, not only will the self remain incomplete, the relationship itself will probably flounder."

Your Thoughts about Others
Create Your Experience of Them

I'm going to ask you to mull over a few statements and reflect on whether you agree with them or not.

1. Just because we think something's true, doesn't mean that it actually is true.
2. Our behavior is driven by what we think is true.
3. Other people have the power to make us feel a certain way.
4. What we get from others is a reflection of what we are giving to them.
5. We can't solve the problem from the same mind-set that created it.

The first of these statements—"Just because we think something's true, doesn't mean that it actually is true"—is one that people often don't have a difficulty with in the abstract. They nod sagely in agreement. However, when they are asked to apply it to something that they hold strong views about, it's an entirely different matter. Take, for example, that colleague at work. You know the one; he's a shirker; a work-shy, lazy so and so. He sucks up to the boss; he's obnoxious and always takes credit for other people's ideas. If I were to suggest that, just because you think that this description of him is true, it doesn't mean that it actually is true, you would immediately put up a defense of your opinion. You'd tell me about all the evidence you have stored away in your memory banks, with dates, times, witnesses and any other proof that I might need to come over to your corner and see things the way that you do. In the abstract, this is a perfectly acceptable idea; but if I ask you to question the validity of the opinions that you've worked so hard to develop, then it becomes less appealing.

Let's try the second statement—"Our behavior is driven by what we think is true." Again, I suspect that is a fairly benign proposition—in the abstract. If I were to ask you what you were thinking that made you fly off the handle at your teenage son over the breakfast table this morning, you would delight in telling me exactly what he did to make your blood boil. "Ah," I'd say, "I'm not talking about what he did; I'm talking about what you thought about what he did, because you've agreed with me that it's what you think is true—in this case about how your son behaved—that made you mad." You might want to hit me at that point. But if you mull it over for a moment, you'll recall that you thought he was out of line because he "should" have gotten up earlier so that he'd be ready when you had to leave for work: but because he stayed up late, playing computer games, he slept in. And that's just selfish. And wouldn't everybody think that? And it's ridiculous that he made you late, and angry. And he should know better. And you've had this conversation with him a thousand times before. That's what you think is true. In fact, that's what you know is true. Of course, you, reacting in the way you did, were driven by your thoughts; your view about what your son ought to have done and your evaluation of the predicament that you were put in because of his actions. It's those evaluative thoughts that made you feel the way you did, and then made you act the way you did. That also deals with statement number three. And four. And you should bear in mind number five if you are hoping to go home tonight to deal with the issue of your teenage son and how he might behave differently.

An Example of How Relationship Dynamics Can Operate

"What we see depends mainly on what we look for."
—**Sir John Lubbock**

Whenever two people interact in the context of a relationship, a dynamic will develop. That dynamic will become more established over a period of time, and eventually, responses will become automatic, and perceptions, expectations and preconceptions embedded.

Let's examine the identity subsets that can exist in a relationship between two people when they do not lead the relationship with themselves. This applies to romantic relationships, friendships, family connections, interactions at work and any other relationship that involves regular dealings between two or more people. Left unchecked, each of us has at least two identities: the one we like to keep hidden ("hidden identity") and the one we want to project to the world ("external identity"). Scientific research shows that we begin to form an impression of a person whom we have just met within three to five seconds of first setting eyes on them. Let's call the view that we form of another the "viewpoint identity." In essence, we have these three identities within each relationship we are engaged in when we fail to lead the relationship with ourselves. In close and loving romantic and family relationships and in friendships, we may disclose more and more of our hidden identity. However, much of our hidden identity is subconscious; we may believe that we are unlovable unless we are perfect, and strive to make our external identity perfect—and correct all the time—so that we can be lovable within the context of the relationship. The need to be right or perfect will, of course, create tension in the relationship. If we do not work hard to notice our thinking and adopt more constructive conscious-thinking patterns— such as "I am enough as I am" or "So what if I'm wrong; what's the worst thing that can happen?"—we will end up in conflict with the external or hidden identity of the other person.

Let's look at an everyday example of how the hidden, external and viewpoint identities might play out.

Amy works as an accountant in a medium-size accountancy firm. She is a senior manager in the tax department and has worked closely with the partner, Trevor, for six years. Trevor is a workaholic, and Amy feels that she needs to be available to work into the evening, just in case Trevor needs her to deal with a piece of client work. Amy partly resents the toll that such long working hours takes on her personal life, but she is a perfectionist and believes strongly that working hard is a virtue. Trevor decides to hire a more junior assistant to work in the team. Amy is not involved in the hiring decision or in the selection of the successful candidate, Samantha, and is resentful about her exclusion from that process. Samantha has worked for one of the very large accountancy firms, and everyone Amy has ever met from that background has been confident in their own abilities. Amy's external identity— the one she likes to project to others—is that she is clever, organized, a great communicator and able to build great client relationships. Amy delivers work on time and to a high standard and is available whenever Trevor needs her. Amy's hidden identity is that she is not good enough. She worries that everything she does might not be "up to scratch," and so works long and hard on projects to make them as perfect as they can be. She looks for Trevor's approval constantly, but he never gives her any feedback.

When she first meets Samantha, who is attractive and smartly dressed, Amy projects her external identity by being bubbly, friendly and helpful. The viewpoint identity that she initially forms of Samantha is of someone who is very confident and self-assured, and she immediately worries that her place in the team as Trevor's "number two" might be under threat. That viewpoint identity is further reinforced over the coming weeks as Trevor delegates work directly to Samantha, without involving Amy. When Trevor asks Amy to do a presentation to the wider team, she does not involve Samantha in preparing or delivering it, even though Samantha is junior to her, and may have had experience in her old firm that would provide some useful content. That is because Amy is starting to view Samantha as "competition."

Whenever Amy imagines delivering the presentation to the wider team, she pictures herself stumbling and stuttering through it and Trevor being disappointed with her, wishing that he had given it to Samantha to do. Amy is allowing her subconscious thinking to be dominated by the thoughts associated with her hidden identity rather than focusing on the strengths she has—and displays regularly. Amy also fails to see how her viewpoint identity concerning Samantha is infecting her thinking and the relationship dynamic that is evolving between herself and Samantha.

Samantha's external identity is that she projects confidence, is articulate and charismatic. Samantha's hidden identity is that she is not clever enough. Samantha was relieved to get the job with this accountancy firm because she hated the large corporate environment that she used to work in, where every assistant was vying for the approval of the managing partner. The viewpoint identity that she has formed regarding Amy is that, initially, she was bubbly and friendly, but has now "frozen her out." She is seeing the same sort of behavior in Amy that she saw in her old colleagues. Samantha has therefore, subconsciously, decided that it is not safe to trust Amy and has distanced herself from her. She works directly for Trevor and worries constantly that the work she is producing is not good enough. Trevor does not give her any feedback, and so she is feeling increasingly insecure and isolated, which has caused her to be more focused on projecting her external identity as confident so that her insecurity does not show, but the effect is rather strained. She knows from her experience at her old firm that showing any lack of confidence can be seen as weakness. When she becomes aware that Amy is doing a presentation to the wider team, she is disappointed not to have been involved either by Amy or Trevor. She decides to learn a bit about the topic so that she can ask some interesting questions and show that she is worthy of being involved in such an endeavor.

At the presentation, Amy notices that Samantha does not look interested. Then at the end of the presentation, Samantha asks a question to which Amy does not know the answer. Amy is livid.

From the example, we can imagine how Amy now feels about Samantha, and how difficult it might be to create a constructive relationship between the two of them. They have each adopted a fixed viewpoint identity about the other and are at the mercy of their fearful thinking which is causing them to cling desperately to their external identity in an effort to hide who they—subconsciously—believe they really are.

Sadly, in Amy and Samantha's case, as their confidence bleeds away, and they fail to take the lead in the respective relationships with themselves and with one another, we can imagine how the rivalry between them is likely to grow and infect the effectiveness of the team. Unfortunately,

Trevor's apparent leadership style (based on my viewpoint identity of him!) appears unlikely to positively contribute to the team dynamic.

Much of what Amy and Samantha were thinking was based on preconceptions and expectations and their own respective subconscious programming.

Psychological Triggers and Effects

Our subconscious mind's programming, unless we change it by leading the relationship with ourselves, will cause us to react to others according to our conditioned responses and habitual-thinking patterns. In essence, that means that we will respond emotionally, in a predetermined way, when faced with certain behavior that our subconscious mind "recognizes" or feels threatened by. That recognition may relate to a particular tone of voice, or word or body language. We feel judged, and because our core—unmanaged—belief is that we are unlovable unless we are perfect, we will feel instinctively defensive. The subconscious mind may recognize, in a moment, an intonation that triggers fear; that recall is something we are not consciously aware of. We often become aware of it only at the point when we feel the emotion of fear. Most of us trust our emotions, without checking whether they are an appropriate response to what we have just experienced—unless we have developed habits consistent with leading the relationship with ourselves. For example, Amy feels livid and is unlikely to question whether it's an appropriate response to Samantha having asked a question. Amy believes she has ample evidence to support her perception that Samantha is trying to undermine her. She is failing to lead in her relationship with Samantha because she is failing to lead in her relationship with herself.

The Bandwagon Effect

The bandwagon effect refers to an individual's tendency to follow the unspoken rules or behaviors of the social group to which he or she belongs. The bandwagon effect is relevant in the context of obtaining a view of an individual from someone whom you perceive knows them well. Imagine that you are inheriting a team, and you ask the outgoing manager (who is leaving the business) to give you the "lowdown" on each of the team members. If you believe that the manager is well informed, then you are allowing him to set your "filter" about each of the team members. That, in turn, leaves you exposed to the risk of confirmation bias. If the manager had a difficult relationship with one member in particular, and you choose to believe what he is telling you about her, that will show in the way in which you behave toward that team member. At a subconscious level, your behavior will indicate to that member of the team that you have taken that view of her; and the unhealthy dynamic which operated previously between her and the manager is likely to be reignited in your own relationship with her. The bandwagon effect will cause you to develop preconceptions—and therefore fixed filters—whenever you blindly rely on the viewpoint of someone you trust or respect. I'm not suggesting that you ignore that viewpoint, but a leader of the relationship with himself would treat it with caution, understanding the fallible nature of it, because of everything he now understands about programming and psychological biases.

Another tendency that can stop us from making conscious choices about our perspective and our behavior is that of deindividuation. Deindividuation is disinhibited social behavior that arises from group experience, resulting in a loss of a sense of individuality. A stark example of this in operation can be seen in the Stanford Prison Experiment, where two groups of students participated in a two-week prison simulation in the basement of a building at Stanford University.[11] Volunteers were prescreened for psychological fitness and were then assigned to one of two groups—guards or prisoners. Guards wore mirrored sunglasses and were instructed to treat prisoners in a particular way, including shackling them. Guards became intoxicated with their power and began taking roll call in the middle of the night, were physically abusive and forced some prisoners to strip naked and to sleep on the concrete floor. The prisoners quickly became demoralized. Sadistic tendencies appeared in some of the guards, and increased as the experiment continued. The depressive, cowering behavior of the prisoners increased too, and the experiment had to be halted six days into the two weeks scheduled for it to last. Some prisoners required counseling for almost a year afterward. The sense of deindividuation that arises when we become absorbed as a member of a group can cause us to "follow the herd" thoughtlessly, unless we remain vigilant and continue to consciously lead the relationship with ourselves.

Nonverbal Communication
The communication studies carried out by Albert Mehrabian, professor emeritus of psychology at UCLA, are often incorrectly overstated. However, those studies did produce two interesting conclusions. Firstly, that there are three elements to any face-to-face communication: words, tone and nonverbal behavior; secondly, that the nonverbal elements are the most important for communicating attitudes and feelings, especially when there is an inconsistency between the three elements.[12] When the tone and nonverbal behavior is inconsistent with what is being said, people tend to believe the tone and nonverbal signals rather than the words. According to Mehrabian, the three elements will contribute to our liking and trusting of a message about a person's feelings and attitude (given to us by that person) to the following extent: words account for 7 percent, tone of voice accounts for 38 percent and body language for 55 percent. Accordingly, for effective and meaningful communication about feelings and attitude, these three elements of the message must be congruent, otherwise we won't really listen to the words; rather, the true meaning will be construed from the tone and body language.

Whereas our words can be consciously selected, our tone and body language tend to be an expression of what we truly believe. Imagine that the manager I referred to earlier told you that the team member applied for your job, but didn't get it, and is now out to undermine you. The team member has picked up some negativity from your body language and asks you if there is an issue. You say, "I don't have a problem with you," in a flat tone of voice while avoiding eye contact. The team member is unlikely to have gained any reassurance from your response—in fact, you've probably reinforced her belief that you don't value or like her. That will be the filter through which she experiences your leadership. Confirmation bias will take care of the rest, because how she behaves will convince you that she is out to undermine you.

Are You a Follower or a Leader of Relationships?

Chances are that your answer to the title question of this section is that sometimes you are a follower and sometimes you are a leader of relationships with others. If I were to ask you what the reason for that variation is, you might initially say that the change in approach depends on who the other person in the relationship is. Now, I'd further question you on that answer if I were your coach. After all, why should your approach about being a leader or a follower alter based on who the other person in the relationship is?

Let me remind you of the five statements set out earlier in this chapter.

1. Just because we think something's true, doesn't mean that it actually is true.
2. Our behavior is driven by what we think is true.
3. Other people have the power to make us feel a certain way.
4. What we get from others is a reflection of what we are giving them.
5. We can't solve the problem from the same mind-set that created it.

We haven't specifically tackled statement number 3 yet. You may agree with it—or you may want to qualify it by adding, at the end, "if we let them." If you have developed the habit of leading a relationship with yourself, you will already have discovered that other people have the power to make us feel a certain way only when we fail to lead our internal response to how they behave. If you reflect on the five statements from the perspective of being a person who firmly leads a relationship with herself, then I'd expect you to agree firmly with each of the statements except number 3—because you'd at least want the qualifier attached to it. If you've reached the point of downright disagreement with statement number 3, then—wow!—you are more than ready to learn how the habits you've ritualized will be invaluable in leading relationships with others.

CHAPTER 6

BECOMING THE LEADER OF YOUR RELATIONSHIPS WITH OTHERS

"You may not control all the events that happen to you, but you can decide not to be reduced by them. . . . If you cannot make a change, change the way you have been thinking. You might find a new solution."
—**Maya Angelou**

Taking the Lead

It Takes Courage

It takes courage, vision and positive expectation to take the lead in a relationship: the courage to break the patterns that have been keeping you stuck in the current dynamic and your existing

89

thinking, the guts to admit that what you believe about the other person might just be wrong. If you are unable to accept that your thinking is mistaken, then reflect on whether it is serving you or them if it is keeping you both stuck in a dynamic that is uncomfortable and frustrating. You need a vision to inspire in you the confidence to know that the relationship could be different. Ask yourself: Who am I capable of being in this relationship? Perhaps you see yourself as an inspiring friend who enables the other person to break out of his or her self-imposed limits and become the best that they can be, rather than feeling like they never take your advice. Maybe you can imagine yourself as a person who is confident and articulate in every interaction with your boss, rather than feeling like he or she has already "written you off." Your courage and vision need to be supported by a positive expectation that you have the ability to influence the behavior of others by engaging with them differently and with a passionate belief that your vision will be realized. These positive expectations apply in your relationships with others, just as they apply in leading a relationship with yourself.

Relationships don't work without work. If you are prepared to do the graft, just as you did through part one, you will enjoy the fruits of your labor. In the same way as you have changed your mental landscape by leading the relationship with yourself, you know that by working on your thinking and interactions, you can positively influence the dynamic in any relationship, once you make the commitment to be the leader of it. If, until now, all your energy has been directed at moaning about how things should be different about him or her or them, then stop. Your "blurting" only focuses your "filter" so that you are guaranteed to get more of what you don't want. Have you ever wondered if the unhealthy dynamic is your fault? What if your insecurities are causing the damage? What if you dissolve every grain of negative association or assumption about the other person, and chose to focus instead on what you could do to improve the relationship? Are you going to direct your energy in this relationship toward high-functioning interaction or away from it? If you care about this connection enough, you will find the courage, vision and positive expectation to lead it.

You Can Even Lead in a Relationship with Your Boss
Being the leader of a relationship does not depend on who sits where in the organizational hierarchy. You are capable of shifting the dynamic in the relationship with your boss just as surely as you can shift it in the relationship with those whom you lead. You may need to use less overt language in doing so, but the beauty of a relationship is that it takes two to tango—the change in the movement of one dance partner has to have an impact on how the other responds. We all exhibit unhelpful behavior to some extent, and making a change alters the trigger that engages unhelpful behavior in another. One small change can start the ball rolling down the hill, building momentum and gathering more goodwill as it travels.

Sudesh was sure that his boss's boss, Mike, thought he was an idiot. He was required to meet quarterly with Mike; and days before the meeting, he would have anxious flashes of how the encounter would go: imagining himself becoming tongue tied and Mike scowling disapprovingly at him. The meetings invariably went badly. I worked with Sudesh to help him understand how relationship dynamics work and how his thinking was driving his behavior. Sudesh realized that his contribution to the dynamic wasn't just his negative preconceptions about how the meeting would go but also his characterization of Mike; he imagined him to be ruthless, judgmental and rude. He changed that characterization, using the relationship room technique set out in the appendix, and began to see Mike as having to get so much done that he continually felt under pressure. He also told himself that Mike placed a lot of importance on what other people thought of him and that, in truth, he valued the role that Sudesh fulfilled. That altered characterization had a material impact on how he felt when preparing for his next meeting. He was no longer focused on what Mike thought of him, but rather on how he could help make Mike's life easier. The trick here is that Sudesh didn't actually need to "know" whether or not much of this information was true; he chose to believe that it was true because it was helpful in his making preparations for the meeting. He preferred to believe Mike valued him, because that belief enabled him to behave as if he was valuable. Sudesh preferred to believe that Mike wanted—and deserved—to be liked and respected because that made it easier to imagine him as fallible and, therefore, worthy of compassion. He used the relationship room visualization (see appendix) to develop that chosen thinking into a habitual-thinking pattern.

Let Go of Those Preconceptions

Think Before You Speak

We are able to powerfully lead a relationship with another only if we have mastered the empowering habits that enable us to lead a relationship with ourselves. If you have mastered those, then the confidence, self-compassion and self-assurance that you already feel will be the portal through which you will easily and dramatically be able to alter any unhealthy relationship dynamic. If you want to lead in a relationship that is—in your current thinking about it—a problematic one, then the first step is to let go of any ideas that you have about the relationship, just as you let go of the programming about your self-identity that disempowered you. Start leading the relationship with an entirely blank slate—as if you were meeting the person for the first time, recognizing that you have created your own experiences of the other person through how you have thought about them.

Imagine that you are about to make a call to your older sister. You'd describe the current relationship as "difficult," and you're calling her only because you will get grief from her if you don't. You see her as negative, and she always criticizes or finds fault with you. With a heavy heart, you pick up the handset and dial her number. Stop right there!

How is this call going to go from your current perspective? Your filter is fixed, and your expectations are primed. Your tone of voice at the beginning of the call will, quite literally, set the tone for the conversation, as your sister—like most of us—will follow your lead in this interaction.

The difficulty with anticipatory emotions is that they arise from what we think a person is going to say or do. That mental filter will determine what we notice, and our anticipatory emotions are written all over our face—or in our tone of voice—and will tend to get the reaction we were expecting in any event. The problem with reactive emotions is that they arise because of the interpretation we have placed on what we have just experienced from a person. The experience has been processed through a mental filter that has attached judgment and created the emotional reaction in us. Letting go of our thoughts about who the person is, what they are going to do or say, what their motivations are and simply being with them in the moment to moment of an interaction is a critical starting point. It means being present and curious about what he or she is going to say or do—each moment unclouded by what has gone before. It's much simpler to put into practice than you might imagine and is an energizing way to interact.

Think of the challenges your sister has, the pressures she may be under. Allow your compassionate inner voice to talk warmly to you about her. Allow your devil's advocate to challenge your current thinking and replace it with understanding and positive expectation. Be determined to stay present during the call and notice, with amusement, if you feel "triggered" by anything your sister says—because you have already cultivated the habit of watching your thinking in leading the relationship with yourself. Now you're good to go. Pick up the handset and make the call, and just see what a difference your fresh perspective has made.

Confirmation Bias
Confirmation bias is the tendency that influences all of us to have more faith in information that is consistent with what we already believe—our perceptions and preconceptions—and to discount opinions or information that disagrees with our beliefs.

The renowned investor Warren Buffett has always been deeply conscious of the role that confirmation bias may play in making unwise investment decisions and says of it. "Charles Darwin used to say that whenever he ran into something that contradicted a conclusion he cherished, he was obliged to write the new finding down within thirty minutes. Otherwise, his mind would work to reject the discordant information, much as the body rejects transplants. Man's natural inclination to cling to his beliefs, particularly if they are reinforced by recent experience, is a flaw in our makeup."

To minimize the effect of this "defect" in our thinking, we can do two things. Firstly, be aware of the danger of confirmation bias and acknowledge that our judgment can be clouded by it; and secondly, enthusiastically seek out and understand information that disagrees with our existing beliefs rather than arguing our own point.

In chapter 5, because of confirmation bias, Amy immediately jumped to a conclusion as to why Samantha asked the question during the presentation. If Amy had sought genuinely to understand the reasons behind the question, she may well have opened up a conversation which could have allowed the growing hostility to melt away and a collegiate bond to form. It's worth remembering that our instinctive tendency is to make up what we don't know, and we conjure up an explanation that coincides with the story that we are already telling ourselves. To "enthusiastically seek out information that conflicts with what we believe" is a big ask; I know. When we recognize a thought or an emotion that has been triggered—now that we appreciate how mistaken it might be—it's critical that we at least reflect on whether it's helpful. We can consciously choose to replace a thought that we have become aware of, and which we know may contribute to an unhelpful relationship dynamic, with a new thought that is going to enable us to give more generously to the interaction. You now have significant experience in using a process just like this—when leading the relationship with yourself. The first rule of habit formation requires us to positively state the new thought in toward language. Here is a tale of how negatively stated outcomes trigger negative subconscious responses because our brain cannot process the syntax in the instruction.

Many years ago, I was coaching a call center manager named Maggie. She had an issue with Joe, a member of her team. She arranged to have a meeting with Joe to discuss some issues that she believed she had with him. She was nervous about the meeting because she was not generally comfortable with conflict and felt sure that Joe was likely to become defensive and belligerent when she began to give him feedback. She entered the meeting room—joining Joe who was already seated—no doubt "leaking" her discomfort all over the room. Joe's body language indicated to Maggie that he was feeling a little apprehensive. Her way of comforting him was to say, "I don't want you to feel uncomfortable. I'm not going to have a go at you. There's no need for you to feel defensive." What Joe's subconscious mind heard was: "uncomfortable," "have a go," "defensive." The meeting did not go well, no doubt largely because negative filters had been reinforced in Joe at the outset, and Maggie had failed to "control her state" and her thinking. It was going to be virtually impossible to rescue a good outcome from such an unpromising start.

Right now I'd like you *not* to think of an elephant, about five feet tall, wearing an oversized pink bow tie with yellow polka dots on it. I imagine it's virtually impossible for you to avoid developing the picture of that elephant in your mind. Your brain conjures up the image even though I am asking you not to, because our brains cannot process the syntax in the instruction. It is, therefore, critical to say what you mean in positive language in both your internally and externally focused dialogue. Maggie could have taken time to fully manage her state (more about this later) and then could have used positive language that focused on what she did want rather than on what she didn't want, such as, "Joe, thanks for coming along. There are a couple of things I'd like your view on so that we can decide on a way forward."

Let's go back to that troublesome person at work, Hugh. Just seeing his name in the sender profile of an email might be enough to make your blood boil. You don't even need to open the email—you already know what he will have written in it. That is a habitual-thinking pattern—a "track" through your mental forest. As soon as you see his name, your brain takes the path of least resistance to what you already know to be true about this person—he's an irritating idiot. You can't simply develop a new habitual response such as writing politely back to him, telling him what you agree with and begging to differ on the remainder of the points he makes. Those words will be typed through a seething veil of irritation, with thoughts firing as you type in each word, reminding you that this guy really is an idiot. Hence, the resulting email will appear to be sarcastic and patronizing. Instead, you can choose to overwrite the existing software programming about who you believe he is, with new programming so that the old thought patterns disappear, in the sense that they become progressively weaker and eventually hold no "truth" for you—and will cease firing in response to seeing his name. You may wonder what benefit the effort of developing new habitual thinking about Hugh might bring you. The current "story" is not serving you—or him. It's perpetuating an unhelpful relationship dynamic. By changing your thinking, you change how you feel and how you behave, and you become more able to positively influence a change in Hugh's behavior. Waiting for him to make the change, without any effort on your part, is useless. You may be muttering under your breath right now—arguing the case for sticking to your view of Hugh because it's, well, true. Please remember your RAS—that filter that has been slowly distorting what you notice about Hugh during the evolution of your relationship with him. It's hard to admit that we may have created our own reality about the identity of a person. The only way that we will know for sure is to wipe the slate clean of all our preconceptions, be conscious of our perceptions and let the relationship dynamic build from there.

The Leading Relationship Mind-Set

Those who take responsibility for leading the dynamic in a relationship believe that, while they cannot control how another person thinks, feels or behaves, they can influence those factors. In fact, they accept the proposition that they do influence the thoughts, feelings and behavior of others regardless of whether they consciously take responsibility for leading the dynamic in that relationship or not. It is that belief that will enable them to think creatively about how to get the best out of the relationship and how to enable the other to fulfill his or her potential.

Presence Is Vital in Leading a Relationship

Our thoughts swing from past to future and back again—seldom are we able to remain in the present for very long, unless we have cultivated the habit of mindfulness. For those who are committed to leading a relationship, the present is the place where the dynamic is altered, just as it is the place where we are able to listen to our own authentic wisdom. In the present moment, there is no assumption that the individual is about to behave in a particular way, because that would be focusing on the future. Nor is there irritation about what they said last week, because that would be focusing on the past. Rather, there is a focus on what the individual is saying or doing, with an attitude of curiosity. We allow the dynamic to unfold rather than to be pushed or pulled in a particular direction by expectation or assumption. We honestly don't know what the other is thinking; how can we, therefore, know what acts those thoughts will give rise to? It can be interesting to see what happens when we least expect it. And if we focus on being present and curious, then that creates a warmer and more welcoming space for the other to engage in.

Appreciating Another's Positive Points

Gratitude can play an enormously powerful role in creating a positive relationship dynamic. In leading the relationship with yourself, you learned to develop a compassionate inner voice so that you could become the best of which you are capable. In the same way, learning to focus on the positive aspects of the other person will generate emotions and behavior which are supportive rather than judgmental. We are so evolved as human beings that we are able to sense insincerity no matter what efforts are made to adapt body language to hide what we are thinking. If we, as mothers, sisters, husbands or friends, have a collection of judgmental thoughts about those whom we care about, then those will drip from our tone of voice and be written all over our face, regardless of the words we use in an attempt to disguise them. Our words may be superficially loving, but every other aspect of our interaction is screaming out what we are really *choosing* to think about who others are.

Making a decision to focus our attention on the challenges they might be facing, or on what may be causing them to behave as they do, and on their positive characteristics creates a harmonious background against which to have a more challenging conversation about your concerns. We therefore create a secure environment that is more likely to breed openness in an individual who would otherwise feel defensive if the judgmental thinking remained.

It's Not You—It's Me

The starting point, then, is an unquestionable acceptance that no one else makes us feel a particular way. Ironically, however, we must also acknowledge that many people cling to the belief that others do make them feel a particular way. It follows that we must accept that our behavior toward others will be relied upon by them as a causal factor for how they feel, and consequently for how they behave, without a ready willingness to take sole responsibility for those factors.

I accept that how I behave will drive how others behave because many people do not accept that they have the ability to exercise conscious choice as to how to respond, even though I believe that no one has the power to make me feel a particular way. Once you accept this apparent contradiction, you're on your way.

Service, Please!

Another helpful "mind-set component" is to accept that, in taking responsibility for leading the relationship, you are there to serve in the growth of another person and to learn what you can from the relationship to enable your own growth. That means, in short, that you will never judge but seek only to understand why another is behaving in a particular way. There is always an explanation: be it a conditioned reflex that you have inadvertently triggered or the failure on your part to make yourself understood. You know, more than anyone, the growing pains you felt in the early days of leading a relationship with yourself when acknowledging your own conditioning and working hard to overwrite it with more empowering programming. The willingness to explore why the relationship or interaction is not working as well as it might will serve as a powerful role model in the relationship, and the other person is likely to mimic this, eventually. The desire to understand must be authentic and not patronizing. The intention is to genuinely get to the bottom of what would make this relationship work better, by observing, correcting, adapting and understanding. No one is at fault. The engine is simply not functioning to capacity— and that capacity will either be 250 cc or 500 cc or turbocharged, depending on the potential of the relationship. Your job is to find what components require change in order to make the relationship work to that capacity. It will require fine-tuning of you and of the other person. The fine-tuning is an iterative process that will happen behavior by behavior. It will not be achieved by you reading out the list of the other person's malfunctions that you have come up with, nor by you taking full responsibility for things not working as well as they might. What I have found is that magic happens when we take responsibility for leading a relationship, and we can never forecast in advance the steps that will be taken toward a fully functioning and rewarding relationship that results from those steps.

No Place for the Ego

When we take responsibility for leading in a relationship, there is no place for our sense of self-importance, even if we are higher up the organizational hierarchy or fulfilling a parental role. Indeed, we may be the most important person, hierarchically speaking, within the organization, but the true measure of a person is the lack of any need on his part to exert his ego over another. Our ego is necessary; it is healthy in relationships to set boundaries and balance our respective needs, and that requires an element of ego. Without ego, we would allow our needs to be subsumed by those of another, and our boundaries would be nonexistent. However, the exerting of our ego over that of another is to disrupt the balance. It is like saying, "I am more important than you." Others may come to the relationship seeking to exert their egos over you, and if you respond instinctively to that behavior, then you are likely to become quickly embroiled in a battle of the egos. Instead, listen carefully so that you can understand fully what interests they are trying to protect, what they may be afraid of or what needs they may have, and deal with them at that level. Keep your ego at bay.

Be Powerless

For those who are conducting relationships from a position of power—that is, power gained by virtue of their position in an organization or environment—be wary. That power can make people do strange things, both to the people who hold the influence and those who are dealing with them. Power can make others inappropriately deferential or defiant. Either way, that creates an unhelpful dynamic. If you hold the power, you hold the responsibility to use it conscientiously, and you have the advantage of moving the relationship onto a healthy footing quickly in demonstrating that you intend to do so. By giving people the opportunity to speak, actively listening when they do so, acknowledging how they feel, agreeing with them when you can and delicately dealing with areas of disagreement, you are showing them respect. It goes without saying that you must be authentic, but I've said it anyway.

In your personal relationships, you may be faced with a situation where an older sibling or longstanding friend believes they have "power" because that is the way the relationship has historically worked. It's helpful to (internally) acknowledge your part in enabling that dynamic to continue, for whatever reason. Historically, it will doubtlessly have been fulfilling a subconscious need of yours—such as the need to feel safe or to "belong"—but now that you are leading the relationship with yourself, that need no longer exists because you are able to meet it yourself. There are a couple of ways to tackle this change. The first is head-on, by having the conversation in which you tackle (gently) what needs to change (from your perspective). (Using the techniques you'll find in chapter 8 will help with that.) The second is by leading the relationship using the preconception and appreciation mind-set approaches set out above.

Control Is the *C* Word

Some years ago, I was sitting on a commuter train when the mobile phone belonging to the man sitting next to me rang. He answered it, having checked the caller ID. His greeting to the caller was warm and loving, and I immediately assumed that it was either his wife or daughter calling him. However, within seconds, he said, "No, you're wrong. You're just wrong." His tone of voice was level, but very controlling, almost dictatorial, and he continued to bluntly tell whoever was on the call that they were wrong. I could, by now, hear the sound of a screaming female voice coming from the receiver. The call did not end well. On my travels, I have heard a hundred telephone calls just like that one. Whether it's husbands "telling" wives or vice versa, "important executives" exerting control over colleagues, I'm never sure whether the protagonist is playing the control up or down, because they are talking on the phone in a public place. The eavesdropping leaves me feeling sad and frustrated, though thus far, I have been able (albeit with difficulty) to restrain myself from interfering.

Such a controlling approach only quells opposing viewpoints in the short term. The emotional impact festers and builds and will invariably reemerge in some other form, such as by relationship breakdown, bust-up, resignation (literal and figurative) or the eventual release of pent-up fury.

The model used in transactional analysis (TA) is useful in helping us to understand what response controlling language is likely to trigger, and how to lead a relationship by pulling the other person from a tendency to use controlling words and behavior toward a more respectful style of communication. TA therapy was founded by Eric Berne in the late 1950s and is based on the theory that each person has three ego states: parent, adult and child. These are used along with other key transactional analysis concepts, tools and models to analyze how individuals communicate and to identify what interaction is needed for a better outcome. TA suggests that we shift between the three distinct ego states of parent, adult and child. The parent state is where we think, feel and behave based on how our parents and other authority figures behaved. When we are in adult state, we think, feel and behave in response to the here and now and are able to draw on our full life experience. In that state, we are generally able to make an objective and realistic appraisal of our life experiences. In the child state, we think, feel and behave just as we did in our childhood.

We move between these ego states all the time. It is not the case that adult is "good" and parent and child are "bad." We change states according to the events, memories and thoughts that we experience; some interactions may put us in to our parent state, where we become judgmental, angry or superior. Interactions that trigger thoughts or memories that embarrass us may put us into our child state, where we might feel ashamed and think that we are bad. States change in response to how other people behave. If you are late attending a meeting at work, and walk in with a Starbucks coffee cup in hand, your boss might slip into parent state and say, "Glad you could join us after you'd got yourself a cup of coffee." The tone and content of the comment is coming directly from his controlling parent. You may respond by saying, "I'm sorry" in a tone of voice that shows you are embarrassed, and your body language may express an attempt to make yourself "small" by taking your seat as quickly and quietly as you can. That would be your adaptive-child state. This transaction is described as *complementary* in TA terms, because a reciprocal transaction has been set up that could be maintained indefinitely. However, it is also an example of where you have allowed yourself to be "led" in the interaction, rather than taking the lead.

Not all transactions are complementary. In the scenario described in the previous paragraph, if, instead of apologizing, you responded by saying, "How dare you—I had a fender bender on the way to work, and I needed the coffee to calm my nerves!" you would also be responding in controlling-parent state. The initial comment made by your boss was a parent comment aimed at your child; but rather than responding in your child state, you responded as controlling parent with a feeling of outrage. Again, you have allowed yourself to be "led" in this interaction, quite by instinct. This is called a *crossed interaction* in TA terms. Unlike complementary transactions, crossed interactions are highly unstable, and one of two things will happen: either the interaction will stop, or there will be a shift in ego states of one of the parties. For example, your boss may apologize, and ask if you are okay—moving to adult ego state. You may respond by saying, "That's okay, how were you to know. I'm fine, thanks, though my car isn't," also in adult state, and so the transaction has become complementary.

How might TA help us to lead the relationship with someone who has a tendency to behave in controlling-parent state? If we don't take the lead, we know that our own controlling parent or adaptive child is likely to be triggered, and that complementary transaction, being stable, will be maintained. The goal of TA therapy is often to strengthen the adult state. When we focus on the characteristics of our adult state—what we naturally become when we are leading the relationship with ourselves—we are able more easily to remain or return to that state in the face of parent or child behavior displayed by another. By remaining in adult, we cause the transaction to be unstable, which means that the individual will behave, ultimately, in a way that is complementary to our adult—by adopting adult behavior. The complementary adult-to-adult transaction is stable and constructive. We are thereby able to lead the relationship to a more constructive and equal dynamic by resisting the pull of the instinctive dynamic and focusing on maintaining our adult state.

This section is not intended to constitute an exhaustive exploration of the fascinating field of TA, but rather to set out some of the key concepts with a view to using those to assist us in being able to lead a relationship. particularly in the face of controlling-parent behavior—though it works equally well for adaptive-child behavior too. For those interested in finding out more about TA, you may wish to read *Staying OK*, by Amy and Thomas Harris.[13]

Forgiveness is the *F* Word
If you are holding on to any grudges, justified though they may be, then this relationship is not going to change. You are choosing to keep it stuck in the debit/credit arrangement that reprisal and retaliation trade in. Forgiveness is a very difficult concept when you're stuck in the retribution mind-set, but it is the only way for you to find peace and make progress in the relationship—just as you did by exercising self-forgiveness when leading the relationship with yourself. Leaders of relationships understand that forgiveness is ultimately a selfish act because it gives the forgiver peace and frees him from the clutches of a past misdeed. Chances are that the offense that you are mulling over was a one-off, but it holds you in its grasp so that you play it over and over in your mind. The other person may have injured you only once, and yet you are choosing to wound yourself again and again. Psychologists define forgiveness as a "conscious, deliberate decision to release feelings of resentment or vengeance toward a person or group who has harmed you, regardless of whether they actually deserve your forgiveness." I am not suggesting that when you forgive, you deny the seriousness of an offense

against you. Forgiveness does not mean forgetting, nor does it mean condoning or excusing an offensive action. Though forgiveness can help repair a damaged relationship, it doesn't obligate you to reconcile with the person who harmed you. In the context of leading relationships, I am applying the principle of forgiveness to a relationship that you are either required or wish to continue with, and so reconciliation will be in order. It may be a relationship at work where the right thing to do for the organization is to have an explicit conversation about what happened in order to fully understand the actions of another to be able to forgive them, and move on. It may be in the context of a friendship which is so dear to you that you have made the decision that you want to continue to enjoy the bond, and therefore, need to move past what has happened. Forgiveness brings the forgiver peace of mind and frees her from corrosive anger. Even if there is no intention to continue with the relationship, the forgiver has freed herself from the thinking that kept her stuck in the rumination cycle.

Be the Person You'd Want to Have a Relationship With

Those who emit a positive energy are inspiring to be around. We feel charged after spending time with them. Those who demonstrate a genuine curiosity in who we are can make us feel remarkable. Dale Carnegie was once quoted as saying: "You can make more friends in two months by becoming interested in other people than you can in two years by trying to get other people interested in you." The more you enable others to talk about themselves, the more fascinating you become! We all have our down days, of course. But the rest of the time, we have a clear choice about whether to express ourselves positively and constructively or whether to be the person who drains everyone's energy. Leaders of relationships understand that they set the tone and the tempo for the interaction. There have been times when I have been determined to go on the charm offensive and move someone's mind-set from irritation to cooperation. One such example is a recent meeting that I had scheduled with a managing director of a large company to discuss the progress of development work I was carrying out with some of the key people in the organization. The human resources director and I were in the meeting room, having both arrived on time; the managing director was late. When he did arrive, he gave me the impression that he was irritable and disinterested and, frankly, would rather have been anywhere but at this meeting. He was gruff and sullen and barely acknowledged us as he entered the room. I immediately put up my "blurting screen" so that his energy wouldn't pull me into a negative thought cycle. I then thought of how grateful I was that he had been so supportive of this project and how important he felt it was. I deliberately focused on the present moment and was curious about how he would behave. I was determined to really enjoy being in his space and learning what I could from him. I smiled warmly. I noticed that he seemed intrigued, perhaps because he didn't get the "reward" that he was used to receiving when he behaved in this way. I asked an open question and listened actively to the response, wanting to learn what I could about the direction he'd like to take in the meeting. I was completely tuned in to him. I felt warmth toward him. It turned into a great meeting. The human resources director asked me how I had turned him around. I hadn't—I'd just not allowed his behavior to drive mine nor "fed" his behavior with his subconsciously anticipated rewards such as becoming meek and deferential. I had simply taken responsibility for leading the dynamic in the meeting.

Stop Bitching and Blurting!

If you have something to say, then please tell the person whom it concerns. Gossiping and bitching are destructive and place those who you are bitching to in a terrible predicament of having either to agree with you or alternatively to stand their ground and refuse to engage. Few people choose the latter option. It's hard to build trust when you lack the integrity to take direct action to resolve an issue and instead prefer to bitch about it. After all, the person you are talking to might wonder what you say about them when they're not around. Blurting is the interpersonal equivalent of cotton candy: it's superficially sweet and enjoyable but will rot your relationships. Let me explain exactly what I mean by "blurting." Imagine that you've been sitting at your desk for the last forty minutes, absorbed in a task. Thelma from accounting pops her head over the wall of your cubicle and asks if you've got a minute. Your inner voice is screaming "Nooooo!" but you nod, and gesture for her to sit down in the empty chair you foolishly keep by your desk for "visitors." Thelma begins to moan and grump about an issue that happened this morning, which is the twenty-first time (approximately) that the same issue has arisen with a colleague. She hasn't spoken to the "problematic colleague" about it or taken any positive steps to resolve the issue. By the time she has finished ranting, you are covered in "blurt grunge"; it's all over you, your keyboard and the chair that Thelma was sitting on. She stands up, having reached the end of her tirade and clearly feeling "unburdened." She wanders away from your workspace, light of step. You return to look at your computer screen, but all your positive energy has been sucked out of you by the blurtathon. You pick up your mug and head off in search of coffee. As you reach the coffee machine, you meet Brian, who asks you how you are. He asks the question in the form of a salutation, not actually expecting you to answer it meaningfully. But you do—you tell him all about Thelma and the "problem," and the blurt flies from your mouth, covering poor old Brian and the coffee machine. You feel much better. Brian leaves the coffee machine, head down, and within a few meters meets Karen, who asks him, without expectation of a meaningful answer, "How are you doing?" You get the picture.

I acknowledge that blurting can sometimes be cathartic; it allows you to blow off steam. If you can't live without it, then please find a "blurting buddy" who has given you permission to blurt all over them, and who will force you to think about solutions to the problems you are blurting about. If you find that you are the person being blurted on, then wheel out your "blurting screen" for protection. The delegates on my leadership development programs love the blurting screen! Imagine a screen that is transparent so that, if you place it between you and the person who is blurting all over you, you can visualize the blurt splatting on their side of the screen and sliding down it without infecting your state of mind. You can remain fully engaged, and your energy and motivation will remain unaffected!

You Are More Likely to Be Wrong Than Right

Have you ever had the experience of being absolutely sure you were right, only to discover that, in fact, you were wrong? How did you feel? I imagine that, initially, you were trying hard to hold on to being right; finding an explanation that would mean that no matter how obvious it now is that you were wrong, in fact there was an error—something you didn't know that simply means you reached your view without all the relevant information. Once you've moved from denial, perhaps you have a sense of being a little angry—even with yourself. You may even feel embarrassed or ashamed. We are programmed from a very early age that being wrong is not acceptable. Our education system rewards us consistently for being right, and if we've been named in class for having failed a test, we are mocked and laughed at by our classmates. We believe, in short, that getting something wrong means that there's something wrong with us. However, trusting our internal sense of rightness is not a wise thing to do. Having an attachment to being right can prevent you from dealing with mistakes as soon as you ought to, or from being as open and flexible in your relationships as you might be. If you are prepared to be wrong about what you think of others—in fact, if you are prepared to want to be wrong when your views of others are negative, then that will transform your interactions. Studies show that we incorrectly "read" the motives of intentions of others around 80 percent of the time.[14] That statistic doesn't improve significantly when it comes to our spouses, family members and close friends; we incorrectly "read their minds" 65 percent of the time! Step outside your space of "rightness," be genuinely curious about what the accurate picture is and admit that you don't know. The only way you can be sure of being right is to ask, and then to listen to what you are told.

The Basis of All Great Relationships Is Love

Okay, I know that those of you who operate in a corporate environment might be curling your toes at the very mention of the four-letter word, *love*, but I maintain that, even in a corporate environment, this statement is true. The strongest relationships have at their core a strong affection, whether borne out of deep respect, admiration or having fought many "battles" together. And so, if you want to make a relationship as great as it is capable of being, then you need to find something lovable or worthy of some affectionate regard in the other person. It can be hard; I know. Sometimes, I've resorted to having to imagine what the person's husband or mother might tell me that they love most about the person! That lovable component is the doorway to your compassion and empathy for the other individual. It is the energy with which you will imbue every word, glance and action, that will help transform the relationship into one that might not be perfect, but is as good as you can make it. You have learned to develop your compassionate inner voice in leading the relationship with yourself—and the same dramatic changes will occur in your relationship with others when you find a hook upon which to hang your outward-focused compassion.

By changing your thinking in the ways in which we have talked about, the contours on the map of the relationship alter, just as the map of your own mental landscape altered as you developed empowering thinking habits in leading the relationship with yourself. By forging those new mental pathways and becoming clearer about who you authentically are, your ability to stand strong and yet be flexible in every external relationship increases. Now that you have the "leading relationship" mind-set firmly established, let's look at what skills you might use to forge even deeper connections with others and tackle the bumps on the landscape that will continue to arise as part of a lifetime of relationships.

CHAPTER 7

FORGING DEEPER RELATIONSHIPS—AND HAVING THOSE DIFFICULT CONVERSATIONS

Making a Connection

Listening Fully and Actively

O f all the skills that will forge a deeper connection *and* help you tackle tricky conversations, fully and actively *listening* is the one to be placed right at the heart of them. Do not be fooled by listening's superficial simplicity, and remember, it isn't what we say that counts, it's what others hear. Demonstrating a clear intention to listen and fully hear what is being said is like pouring just the right amount of honey down a sore and swollen throat—it will soothe raspy relationships—just as failing to actively listen will inflame already sore wounds.

Active listening is one of four modes of listening that also includes *deep*, *conversational* and *cosmetic*. The features of cosmetic listening are that you will be sharing a physical space with someone and will be within earshot, but that's about it. While they are talking, you're likely engaged on another task. Imagine the boss who is typing up a report on her laptop when a member of her team knocks gently on the door to her office and asks if he can talk to her for a moment. The terse nod that he receives in response to the request causes him to enter the room nervously and begin to speak. While the team member is addressing his points to his boss, she continues to type, making *mmmm* sounds every now and again to give the impression that she is listening. You may recall that in chapter 1, I mentioned that the limitations of the conscious mind are such that it can only focus on one thing at a time. Therefore, the boss is either focusing on that report she's typing, or she's focusing on what her team member is telling her. She can't do both; it's impossible. Perhaps she's moving from one to the other, switching her conscious attention to what she is being told when a word or two hooks her interest. Either way, she is doing one or both things badly; she will have to go over the section of the report she has just typed again, to make sure it's up to scratch, and she's clearly demonstrating to her team member that what he has to say holds little or no interest for her. Her team member walks away feeling demotivated and unvalued and probably none the wiser about what action he is to take, and the boss has to retype the section of the report again because, well, she couldn't really concentrate. That's cosmetic listening. Please don't try it with anyone you care about.

Conversational listening is the kind that we engage in when having coffee with friends—catching up with each other on the recent ups and downs of life. There's an easy talk-talk, listen-listen rhythm to this type of interaction. We are likely only to remember 50 percent of what we were told, but that's probably okay when we are not expecting to be questioned closely on the detail of it at a later date. However, it's necessary to pay close attention during conversational listening. If your friend's pace of speech slows, and her eyes hold steady on yours, you're likely to be shifting into active-listening territory as she shares with you something meaningful to her.

We engage deep listening when we are looking for what is not being said in the interaction. Counselors and therapists use this kind of listening as their "stock in trade." When we have deep friendships, loving relationships and particularly as parents, we will use deep listening to try to hear what is really meant by what is being said—it involves focusing closely on the tone of voice and body language rather than the words being used by our loved one.

In our busy lives, we tend to default to conversational or even cosmetic listening, and we forget how meaningful it is to give the gift of our full attention to the speaker. We mentally climb over the words, looking eagerly for a gap to squeeze in our story or experience of the topic. Once you are aware of how powerful active listening is in soothing the soul and building a connection, you carry it around like a velvet glove, eager to clothe your attention in it when required because you understand that, often, it's the only way in which we can really help others.

When we are listening *actively*, then that is all we are doing. We are not thinking about what we are going to say next, or reflecting on whether we agree with what has just been said or thinking about the better story that we want to tell. Active listening is about being completely present and of service to the speaker, taking in every word that is being said, with the intention of understanding fully. It takes a huge amount of concentration to actively listen; there's a change in the atmosphere when someone is listening in this way. Time slows down. A connection is made. It is often sustainable only for short periods of time—perhaps a few minutes or so. The focus used for listening actively enables us to allow insights to come through, because the chatter of our mind has been quieted through the active-listening process. I've noticed time and again how the energy created by active listening is enough to encourage others to really open up, even when discussing a topic that they are normally defensive about. It's an effective way of pouring oil over the troubled waters of a difficult discussion.

Raising Tricky Issues and Handling Difficult Conversations

Most of us hate conflict. We avoid having the difficult or uncomfortable conversations because, well, they are just too difficult and uncomfortable. We'd much rather grumble to colleagues about our cranky boss, to friends about our inconsiderate husband and to our neighbors about our other thoughtless neighbors! What if you had the skills to know exactly where to begin to tackle a tricky topic and how to navigate the emotions and challenges that arise during difficult conversations, forging ahead to a clearly articulated outcome?

The Three-Level Assessment

I approach the tackling of tricky issues by determining first of all, how significant the "problem" is in the relationship, using a three-level approach. A level-one issue would include those situations when you have a niggling irritation with someone, and you want to talk to them about what's bothering you, without blowing things out of proportion. In a level-one situation, you appreciate that you may not be seeing things objectively, and the emotional upset that you feel is relatively transitory. Alternatively, a "level two" discussion would be necessary if you have allowed the irritation to fester so that your conversation needs to be more intense—or the behavior of the other person is completely out of line, and you need to talk to them about how you feel. Finally, "level three" would cover the circumstances when there has been a breakdown in the relationship in some way, or there are deep, repeating patterns that need to be worked through in detail.

Level One: The Feedback Mechanism

For a level-one conversation, I would use the feedback mechanism, which is a simple framework that enables you to straighten your thinking before raising the issue, and to frame it in an objective, "light touch" way. The feedback mechanism has three components: "I notice; I imagine; I feel." The first component is useful in forcing you to set out objectively what you saw or heard—what is the behavior or the communication that has caused you difficulty? This is simply a statement of fact rather than opinion. The second component pushes you to work out what assumption or conclusion you have reached as a result of the behavior or communication. The verb *imagine* doesn't sit comfortably with everyone—and if that's the case for you, then you can substitute another in its place—such as "wonder," "assume" or "suspect," as long as those are accompanied by a tone of voice that makes it clear that you aren't certain that the assumption or conclusion is right, and that what you are really doing is checking in to see if it is. The third element, "I feel," is your opportunity to say, in a neutral way if possible, how the behavior or communication has made you feel and what solution you think might make you feel better. As an example, "I noticed that you hadn't contacted me for a couple of weeks. I wondered if I had done something to offend you"—neutral/curious tone of voice. "I felt that it was important to check in to make sure everything is okay. If it is, can we agree to speak more often, because I miss you when we're not in regular contact."

Level Two: Whole Messages

Whole messages can be used for a level-two conversation—when there is a topic that you want to discuss, and you are concerned that it might cause some discomfort for the other person or even lead to conflict.[15] Whole messages describe your observations, thoughts, feeling and your needs, and so have an extra component to the feedback model. A whole message is intended to clearly communicate what you need to say in a reasonable and nonthreatening way. The following are the four components of a whole message.

- Observations—These are statements of fact, things you have experienced, seen or heard. A central feature of whole messages is that your observations are objective and unbiased. Avoid making emotive statements, jumping to conclusions or trying to interpret the other person's motives.
- Thoughts—These are your perceptions and opinions. When you describe your thoughts, you reveal subjective information about how things are from your point of view.
- Feelings—These are statements that describe your emotional response.
- Needs—These are statements describing what you would like to happen. It's important that your needs are not expressed as demands, but as requests or preferences.

I had a recent experience of having to have a level-two conversation that may help illustrate the difference between the feedback model and whole messages. My first signal that something was not okay was a sense of irritation toward a friend of mine who hadn't (to my mind) shown any appreciation for something special that I had done for her. That line of thought took me to other examples over the last year or so, and I realized that I had been doing all the "running" in the relationship.

I went from mild irritation to deep hurt quite quickly when I realized that there was (as I saw it) an embedded pattern of behavior where, in essence, I felt I was always there for her, and she was almost never there for me. The leading relationship mind-set work was not going to solve this problem because my needs were not being met; and therefore, it was my responsibility to raise the issue with my friend. Until we talked about the problem, there was no chance of it being solved. I thought about having a level-one conversation and discounted it because this was not a "one-off" but a pattern that I realized I would need my friend to commit to working with me to change if this relationship was going to survive. It had to be a level-two conversation.

The whole-messages model was incredibly helpful in identifying precisely what the issue was that was making me unhappy and forcing me to communicate in a way that was more likely to lead to a constructive interaction about the way forward. I focused first on my observations of how our respective roles had been playing out in the preceding months. That was a deeper analysis than the first step of the feedback mechanism allows for. I had a number of observations about our respective approaches to the relationship that I worked hard to describe in an entirely objective way.

I then worked out what conclusion I had reached as a result of what I'd observed—that I felt that the friendship was one-sided and, therefore, out of balance. I then checked on how that made me feel, and I realized that I was hurt because I felt that I just wasn't an important part of my friend's life. What I needed fell out easily from that analysis: I needed to know whether there was room for me in her busy life, and whether she wanted to support me in the way I supported her. I realized that aspect was a "deal breaker"—if that need was not met, then I would not be able to remain in the friendship. That's another clear distinction between a level-one and level-two conversation—if there's a "deal breaker" to be discussed, then the feedback mechanism does not provide the level of depth required to build in context to such a deeply felt need. If she was committed to the relationship, then I also wanted actions that spoke louder than words—I needed her to demonstrate that she valued the friendship too. The whole-message model gave me the construct for a whole conversation, and the confidence to do what I could to enable the relationship to be enriched as a result of it, rather than wither on the vine.

Level Three: The GROW Framework

A level-three conversation is required when there has been a breakdown in the relationship of some sort, or there are deep, repeating patterns that need to be worked through in detail.

The GROW framework is a popular model which is used principally in coaching conversations. I have adapted this model, but I will stick with the core acronym which is G for "goal," R for "reality," O for "options" and W for "way forward." Following is a practical example of using the model to raise a friend's awareness about how she may be contributing to a difficult relationship dynamic in her marriage.

Let's imagine that your friend Anna has been complaining to you about her husband for years. The theme of what she complains about is always the same, though the examples of how he has "repeatedly failed her" (as she sees it) change from time to time. Over the years, you've given her lots of advice that she has flatly ignored. You've become frustrated because she never listens to your advice and doesn't really seem to want to solve the problem. You decide that you will use this GROW technique to see if you might finally be successful in helping your friend shift the dynamic in the relationship with her husband.

Your first step is to be clear about the goal—what do you want to achieve from the conversation when you meet her tomorrow for lunch? If you want to help her come to a practical action plan—things that she can do—to start to improve her relationship with Frank, her husband, then that's a clear goal. Please appreciate, though, that the suggested actions she might take to do that, should originate from her. "Telling" her what the solution to her problem is didn't work before, and it's not going to work now. If you are right—that Anna has not really had an appetite to solve the problem previously—then this technique will flush out whether that's true or not and give you an opportunity to set your boundaries for any future discussion. By way of further preparation, you will remind yourself of the themes of the complaints that Anna always makes about Frank. She sees him as thoughtless—he leaves her to do everything around the house, taking no responsibility for feeding or looking after the children, unless she specifically asks him to. He is (apparently) stubborn and will never admit he is wrong. You know from what Anna has told you, that she speaks to him as if he is a child, such is her level of frustration with him, and does so even in front of the children—and that is beginning to undermine their respect for Frank.

When you and Anna meet, the inevitable barrage of complaints begins. You silently remind yourself of the goal in your head—don't share it. Then move to the reality phase of the conversation. This phase is essentially about unpacking all the facts—not just the ones that Anna selectively wants to share with you. You will be conscious of your tone of voice—curious and calm—and clearly concerned. You will be asking open questions (What? When? How? Who?) directed at letting her see all the perspectives in the relationship. As a reminder those are: her *viewpoint* of Frank (she's already giving you that in spades), how she is behaving toward him (her external identity), what she isn't sharing with him (her hidden identity—perhaps that she is hurt that he doesn't care enough to help her, or that she misses the times when they used to work as a team, and that made her feel loved). The other perspectives are: how he is behaving toward her (his external identity), and with a little prodding, you may be able to get Anna to see that what she perceives might not be exactly how he is behaving—as her filter is on high alert.

You will ask her about what he might not be sharing with her (his hidden identity)—this is a very powerful and fertile area for Anna to reflect on, as it may help her see where Frank feels vulnerable or undermined, and may start to prick a trickle of compassion and insight. Finally, you will ask about his viewpoint identity of her—also a potentially fertile line of inquiry: How is he reading her behavior and the fact that she undermines him in front of the children? What harm is that doing to the relationships in the family?

In your past discussions with Anna, it's likely that she was focusing only on her viewpoint identity of Frank and his external identity, and a narrow description of her external identity toward him, and entirely ignoring all the other perspectives in the relationship. By questioning her (gently), you will help shine a light on all four corners of the relationship and help her see things from his perspective. There is also the perspective of the children—but that may be a step too far.

Once you have illuminated the current reality, it's time to move on to options. These are *her* ideas about how to pour oil on these troubled waters, and not yours—no matter how great you think your ideas are. The truth is that Anna will be more invested in her solutions than in yours. So, again, sticking with open questions, ask her how she might approach things differently, what needs to happen to open Frank up to really listening to what she needs, whether there are needs that Frank has that she is not meeting. In short, your questions are directed at finding out what she could do to lead the relationship to a better dynamic. Of course, she needs to lead the relationship with herself first, by challenging her old thinking and the stories she has been telling herself. Your questions about the differing perspectives should prompt her to start examining her shared responsibility in creating the current dynamic.

Once Anna has come up with some options, ask her which ones she feels most comfortable with. Then you're ready for the final step—the way forward. Encourage Anna to say what she will do and by when, and offer to be there to support her if she needs a sympathetic ear. You could even now coach Anna on using the GROW model and the relationship perspectives to have that difficult conversation with Frank. It will be just as effective, and, after your great coaching session with her, she will likely be in a frame of mind where she is prepared to make concessions about how unhelpfully she has been behaving!

Managing Differing Perspectives

It used to be very important to me to be right. I think that being a paid adviser can have that downside: we are paid for our advice, so we must be right. That's not an endearing quality outside the advisory transaction, however. It tended to make me stubborn and unwilling to listen to opposing viewpoints, neither of which is particularly effective in influencing skills or behavior. Once we understand that our thinking can be fallible, that tends to make us more receptive to opposing viewpoints. If our thinking is fallible, then listening carefully to another viewpoint can help us broaden our own thinking. However, we can often be faced with someone whose viewpoint is fixed. If we are aiming to have as healthy a dynamic as possible in our interactions with others, then we have to take responsibility for keeping our own perspective open and doing what we can to open up the outlook of the other person. I've already spoken about the many techniques for influencing the dynamic in an interaction, and those apply equally during a conflict of views. That mind-set will be a helpful backdrop against which to apply some "opening up" techniques.

As before, we start with the objective in mind—what is it that you want to achieve from this conversation? Once you are clear about that, then you will want to understand fully what the other's perspective is. That involves questioning and actively listening to the responses because you have a genuine desire to understand. In responding with your own view, it is critical to do what you can to find any areas upon which you agree. Take the time to explain why you agree. Then, if there are areas where you do not agree, before setting those out, acknowledge that this is just *your* perspective. Normally, all that we are sharing is our opinion of what we think is the right next step or account of what happened. If we acknowledge that it is just our opinion or perspective, then that sends a signal—which will hopefully register—that all we can ever share is our particular point of view because we have experienced it through our thinking. It follows that to state your perspective as a "fact" would be inaccurate; all we can ever do is share what we *think* the facts are. That doesn't change history; it just tells another what we think history looks like. It takes courage to acknowledge that, but it is an incredibly powerful thing to do when there is a clash of views. I've also found that it's almost never necessary to say "You're wrong" or "No"—instead focus on what you are able to accept and give reasons why the alternatives are not acceptable to you. Identifying those interests that you each share and want to protect or pursue will keep the discussion on a constructive track too. However, please note that all these "techniques" will reek of insincerity if you do not genuinely believe that the other person may well be "right" and you may well be "wrong," and if you are not genuinely taking responsibility for leading the discussion to a better resolution for both of you.

CHAPTER 8

MAINTAINING RESILIENCE THROUGH THE TOUGH TIMES: THE QUICK FIX SIX

I know that it isn't always possible to consistently apply all the tools and techniques that we have covered so far, especially in the early days of leading the relationship with others. So, I've created the *six resilience factors* as a shortcut to identifying how to move from being "stuck" to being resourceful and resilient in any situation where you're required to take the lead in a relationship with another.

A Resilient Foundation

Resilience is the ability to recover readily from adversity, which obviously encompasses a spectrum of events, from the traumatic to the trivial. While resilience factors are terrific at maintaining resourcefulness in the face of most adverse situations, they are not intended to be a substitute for counseling or therapy when that support is required to help an individual recover from the most traumatic of events.

The hallmark of resilient people is that of relying principally on their own opinion rather than being hostage to the good opinion of others. Resilient people keenly and consistently lead in the relationship with themselves. They aim to focus on the present moment rather than being pulled back to the past or overly focusing on the future. In order to do that, they have tamed their inner critic and created a constructive inner voice that is supportive and resourceful, casting around for solutions whenever a problem arises. Another characteristic of resilient people is that they like themselves and value the contribution they are making to the world while constantly looking for ways to make that contribution more meaningful.

The Six Resilience Factors

"The only thing missing from any situation
is that in which you are not giving."
—Marianne Williamson

If we learn to ritualize just six habits, then we will be able to maintain our resilience in any situation and lead our internal and external relationships constructively and powerfully. I have found that almost every issue perceived as a relationship problem can be resolved by working on one or more resilience factors during the coaching process. However, once you know what the resilience factors are, you can learn to "coach" yourself, by simply working through each of the factors to check which isn't getting your full attention, work on it and then lead the relationship to a healthier dynamic.

The only thing missing from a situation in which you feel overwhelmed or under pressure is a resilience factor that you are not attending to. The six resilience factors are:

1. Exercising conscious choice.
2. Being aware of your thinking.
3. Maintaining an outlook of realistic optimism.
4. Being clear about needs and boundaries.
5. Exercising understanding instead of judgment.
6. Reaching out for support.

Resilience Factor One: Exercising Conscious Choice
"It's not what happens within a relationship, it's how I deal with it that matters," is the mantra of the relationship leader. The first component of that statement is something that we often cannot control, while the second element is something we certainly can.

A useful model conceived by psychologist Albert Ellis, after he had become frustrated by the approach of traditional psychoanalytic therapy, is set out below. According to Ellis, "people are not disturbed by things but rather by their view of things." His fundamental assertion was that the way people feel is largely influenced by how they think.

The ABC Model
Ellis suggested that people mistakenly blame external events for unhappiness. He argued, however, that it is our *interpretation* of these events that truly lies at the heart of our psychological distress. To explain this process, Ellis developed what he referred to as the ABC model:

- *A* (Activating Event)—Something happens in the environment around you.

- *B* (Belief)—You hold a belief about the event or situation.
- *C* (Consequence)—You have an emotional response to your belief.

In short, *A* does not cause *C*; *B* causes *C*; it's what we believe about what has happened that creates our reaction to it. If we develop the habit of consciously choosing how we will respond to the behavior of another, we hold the power to influence the outcome constructively. Being flexible in the way in which we exercise conscious choice comes from knowing what options are open to us. We are more likely to see the array of options when we understand that the choice is entirely ours.

The very first step in the process is to identify the thoughts and beliefs that lead to our instinctive, emotional response to the behavior of another person. In many cases, these beliefs are reflected as absolutes, as in "I must," "I should," "I can't," or "They should." According to Ellis, some of the most common irrational beliefs include:

- feeling excessively upset over other people's mistakes or misconduct,
- believing that to be valued and worthwhile you must be 100 percent competent and successful in everything,
- believing that you will be happier if you avoid life's difficulties or challenges,
- feeling that you have no control over your own happiness—that your contentment and joy are dependent upon external forces.

By holding such unyielding beliefs, it becomes almost impossible to respond to situations in a psychologically constructive way. Possessing such rigid expectations of ourselves and others leads only to disappointment, recrimination, regret and anxiety.

Once these underlying feelings have been identified, the next step is to consciously choose to release them, appreciating that they do not serve any useful purpose and keep us stuck in an unconstructive mind-set.

Resilience Factor Two: Being Aware of Your Thinking

This aspect follows from appreciating that we can choose how to respond in any given situation. Once we know that to be true, we can explore our thinking about what has happened. As we know, every thought drives an emotion, and every emotion drives action and behavior. If we develop the habit of becoming aware of our thoughts, then we can look at them as an artist might critically observe his work: Are the thoughts I am having about this situation helpful? Is there a way in which I can think about the situation more constructively so that I can lead this relationship to a healthier dynamic? Can I think more charitably about the motives of the other person? There are occasions when only space and time will enable us to change the thinking about the situation to something which is more constructive, and it is important to take that time when we can. The habit of seeing our thinking as separate from who we are, much like the ticker tape that runs along the bottom of a televised news broadcast, enables us to appreciate that our thinking is simply a conditioned mental reflex to the situation we are faced with. Our thinking is based on faulty perceptions of this relationship, and it is helpful to cultivate an attitude of curiosity or amusement as we observe that thinking and reflect on what thinking might be more constructive. The key difference between this resilience factor and the first is that the first is deployed whenever we are faced with an external event that we can then consciously choose to respond to; whereas factor two is perpetual. Because our "mental chatter" rattles on incessantly, the habit of observing our thinking is one that we can apply continuously, until we have developed a habitual sense of detachment from what we think.

Resilience Factor Three: Realistic Optimism

There are many studies on our tendency toward either optimism or pessimism. The good news is that optimism is a mind-set and practice that can be learned and developed. I am not talking about developing a Pollyanna, positive view of the world, but rather adopting an approach that is realistically optimistic and based in the belief that we are often able to shape the outcome in any given situation. I define realistic optimism as "the belief in our ability to make a difference in what we do and how we do it." Positive expectation lies at the heart of realistic optimism.

When I'm working with a group, I think it's really important to learn the names of the individuals within the group before the session begins. That can mean that I have to learn fifty or sixty names within a short period of time if I happen to be working with a large group. Almost without exception, a member of the gathering eventually asks how I manage to remember so many names, and then everyone else in the grouping nods in approval at the question. I ask the individuals if they would like to learn how to memorize forty or fifty names within ten minutes, and they all nod enthusiastically. Then, before sharing my secret, I ask those in the group whether they believe that they can remember more than, say, five or six names at one time. If I'm lucky, one or two hands will go up. If they don't believe they can do it, then they simply won't be able to. We need to convert any negative expectation into a positive expectation, otherwise we'll fall at the first hurdle; and that's the first tip to remembering several names at once. Do you want to know the other two tips? Okay—the second is to be completely present, engaged with and genuinely interested in the people you are meeting. Then—and this is the third tip—when you learn their names, take a moment to create a recall mechanism. My recall mechanism is to think of someone I already know with that name and to visualize that person. If I happen to be meeting someone who has a name I've never encountered before, I might ask the person about it, then take time to picture the word written out or an object that the name reminds me of. Try it—but believe you can do it first!

> *"If I accept you as you are, I will make you worse;*
> *however, if I treat you as though you are what you are*
> *capable of becoming, I help you become that."*
> —**Johann Wolfgang von Goethe**

We are capable of setting expectations in others that will have an impact on the outcomes that they achieve. This is a critically important realization for all of us: those who are parents, mentors or leaders—in fact those fulfilling any role where influence of any kind might be exerted. The first psychologist to systematically study how teachers' expectations of students impact the outcomes that those students achieve was Harvard professor Robert Rosenthal, who, in 1964, carried out an experiment at an elementary school south of San Francisco.[16] The aim of his study was to identify what would happen if teachers were told that certain children in their classes were destined to succeed. Rosenthal took a normal IQ test and dressed it up, giving it the title Harvard Test of Inflected Acquisition. He told the teachers that this very special test from Harvard had the ability to predict which children were about to experience a dramatic growth in their IQ. After the children took the test, he then chose at random several children from each class. There was nothing at all to distinguish these children from the others, but he told their teachers that the test predicted which children were on the verge of an intense intellectual bloom. As he followed the children over the next two years, Rosenthal discovered that the teachers' expectations of these kids really did affect the students. "If teachers had been led to expect greater gains in IQ, then increasingly, those kids gained more IQ," he said.

As Rosenthal did more research, he found that the expectations affected, in a thousand almost invisible ways, teachers' moment-to-moment interactions with the children they taught. Teachers gave the students whom they expected to succeed more time to answer questions, more specific feedback and more approval. They consistently touched, nodded and smiled at those children more than others.

This third resilience factor is about consciously setting expectations in others that are realistically positive. In our drive to help our relationship with others achieve its potential, it's important for us to be consciously aware of the role that our expectations of them will have on how we interact with them, and how that, in turn, will enable them to develop positive expectations of themselves and their relationship with us. Studies have shown that those with higher expectations will work harder to achieve a goal and will project themselves differently. Those people also take a different view of setbacks; they are determined to learn lessons so that they can approach a similar situation differently next time. That is all based on the optimistic thinking that they are able to influence outcomes, and they understand that thoughts create their emotions that, in turn, create their behavior.

Resilience Factor Four: Being Clear about Your Needs and Boundaries

*"The single biggest problem in communication
is the illusion that it has taken place."*
—George Bernard Shaw

Have you ever found yourself thinking, "He should have known," or "She should have told me"? We all have a rulebook that we expect other people to have read. When they break the rules contained in our rulebook, we get angry or frustrated or irritated because, well, they "should" have known. One of our several cognitive tendencies is to believe that others see the world as we do. They don't. If you are talking to a friend who continues to look at her mobile phone while "listening" to you, rather than becoming irritated, tell her that you'd like her full attention. If you feel awkward about making a "fuss," then know that your irritation arises from your lack of courage in asking for what you need rather than your friend's behavior. If you come down to the kitchen in the morning and notice that your husband has not cleared away the dishes from the previous evening, before giving him the silent treatment, ask yourself first, "Was I explicit about what I wanted him to do?" Whenever you feel irritated about the behavior of another, check in with yourself to establish whether you were clear about what you needed, before reacting. Lead in the relationship by taking responsibility for being explicit about what you need, even if you think it's obvious because it's in paragraph fifteen of your rulebook. Unfortunately, telepathy is not yet part of our evolved skill set.

Margaret worked part-time in a demanding role. That meant that even when she left the office at 4:00 p.m. each day to meet her childcare commitments, she often felt she had to continue to be available on her smartphone all evening, checking her emails and dealing with anything urgent that had arisen. That interfered with the quality time she had hoped to spend with her son, and she wondered whether the part-time arrangement was even worth it. She grew resentful of the imposition—as she then saw it—work had on her family time. Margaret had never had an explicit conversation with her boss about these pressures, what was expected of her or how she might balance those expectations with the needs of her family. She hadn't been explicit—even with herself—about her boundaries or her needs. When I encouraged her to have that conversation, it was the first time that she had even thought about setting out her practical needs and how to balance those with the needs of the business. In the end, she felt that she didn't need to have an explicit conversation because setting out her own boundaries, in the form of rules about when she would and wouldn't look at her smartphone, gave her sufficient control.

Is there any area of your life where you haven't been as explicit as you could be about your boundaries and your needs?

Resilience Factor Five: Exercising Understanding versus Judgment
Judgment is often about placing a label on an event or person which makes it/him/her "right" or "wrong," leaving you stuck in the mindset and the emotional repertoire that goes with that label. Seeking to understand requires us to fully establish the facts of what happened, without any preconceptions as to fault that may cause our confirmation bias to operate and miss vital clues in the fact-finding process. The questions appropriate to the process are fact focused rather than blame oriented: "Tell me what happened when . . ." rather than "What did you think of him when he did that to you?" The objective is to move past what has happened and learn from it, rather than remain stuck in a blame bog, where agreement on who is right or wrong is unlikely to be reached. Consensus about how to move on from what has happened is (eventually) much easier to achieve, and that will encourage resilience in others and lead the relationship to a better place.

Melissa thought her boss was out of order. She felt constantly criticized by him and under attack. Melissa felt powerless— if she tried to talk to her boss, it would end in tears. She believed that her boss just shouldn't behave like that—it was plain wrong. Having ruled out the "talking" option, Melissa and I worked out what other options might be available.

Melissa's language about her boss was judgment based, and she insisted that she had plenty of evidence to support her views, if I wanted to hear it. Being "right" was costing Melissa her equanimity. Instead, we looked for reasons why her boss might be behaving in this way, approaching the matter with an open mind and a genuine desire to find out why this might be happening. As we talked, I could see Melissa's perspective soften; she even felt some compassion when she thought about the pressure he was under at work, his on-going divorce and the fact that he missed his children. She remembered a time when he was much more patient and reasonable. She could not excuse his behavior, but she could understand it, and that made her more flexible in her thinking about how she might be able to remove some of the pressure he was facing at work. At our next coaching session, Melissa told me that she had noticed a distinct improvement in their communication and felt optimistic that that would continue.

Sometimes a barrier prevents us from truly enquiring about the motives or intentions behind behavior is that we suffer from the illusion of insight. Friends, workmates and romantic partners think that they know each other's minds better than the minds of strangers. While it's true that we are better able to better read the minds of close friends and loved ones than those of strangers, the margin is not as significant as we might expect. William Ickes, a pioneer in research on mind-reading accuracy, reports that in his experiments "strangers read each other with an average accuracy rate of 20 percent" when videotaped and later asked to report their moment-by-moment thoughts and feelings.[17] He points out that close friends and married couples "nudge that up to 35 percent." The confidence we feel in knowing the mind even of a close friend or loved one far outstrips our accuracy.

Understanding is particularly important when we are in conflict with another person—and that's precisely when we least want to take the time to get to know them better. An experiment carried out in 1999 involving students from two separate universities was aimed at understanding the impact of increased or decreased anonymity on the degree to which conflict escalated.[18] One group from each university (group A) entered into negotiations with each other by email, without having any personal information about the individuals they were negotiating with. Another group from each university (group B) was set up. Those in group B had to reveal information about themselves to the corresponding negotiating team at the other university. They exchanged photographs and short biographies about themselves. They also had to start negotiations by entering into a conversation by email about something that had nothing whatsoever to do with the matter under negotiation. The results of the study were that the "impasse rate" for group A was 29 percent and for group B 6 percent, demonstrating that understanding your "opponent" better from a human perspective helps you change your mind about them and move forward even in a difficult negotiation.

Resilience Factor Six: Reaching Out for Support
Finally, the resilient man—or woman—is not an island. Reaching out is an important step in maintaining resilience. This is about recognizing when you need help and asking for it. When we are in a stressful situation, the "cuddle" hormone, oxytocin, is secreted, which encourages us to look to those we care about for support. You might want to develop a way of thinking differently about something that has happened, or to talk things through, so that you can more readily examine your thoughts. You may be genuinely seeking out an objective viewpoint on the situation. Having someone whose view you trust, and who themselves practice resilience is crucial; the purpose of reaching out is to help you overcome the adversity, not keep you mired in it.

Our Resilience Brain Circuitry

Our resilience circuitry sits at the prefrontal cortex of our brain, which is located near our left temple. There are practical steps that we can take in order to develop our resilience circuitry, such as practicing meditation. In two studies carried out by neuroscientist Sara Lazar, the impact of meditation on the brain's neuroplasticity was explored.[19] The first study involved participants from the Boston area who already practiced meditation on a daily basis for thirty to forty minutes. A magnetic resonance imaging (MRI) scan was taken of their brains, and the results compared with a control group that was demographically matched but did not meditate. The study found that there were several regions of the brain that had more grey matter in the meditators than in the members of the control group. However, there was some concern that factors other than the activity of meditation may be responsible, to some extent, for the differences in the amount of grey matter shown in the MRI scans. A second study was therefore conducted in which a group of volunteers who had never meditated before were subjected to an MRI scan, and then placed on an eight-week program of thirty to forty minutes daily meditation. At the end of the eight-week period, a further MRI scan was taken to track any difference in the brains of the participants. The results were interesting. In the left hippocampus—the part of the brain that assists memory, learning and emotion regulation—there was a growth of grey matter. This confirmed the results of the earlier study that had shown that fifty-year-old meditators had the same amount of cortex as twenty-five year olds in a region of the brain that traditionally shrinks as we get more mature. The second study also looked at the temporo-parietal junction (the section above the left temple) that is important for perspective taking, empathy and compassion—the resilience circuitry—and found that the grey matter in that section of the brain had also increased in the meditators. Finally, the scans showed a decrease in grey matter in the amygdalae, which evidenced a reduction in stress levels of the meditators and confirmed the anecdotal reports made by them that they felt less stressed as a result of having meditated.

When the need to be resilient arises, then it is important to be focused on the moment so that you are able to become an objective observer of your thinking and the events going on in the room rather than be a hostage to your emotions. I am not suggesting that it is wrong to feel; we know, though, that our feelings are often not an appropriate response but rather driven by some old programming that no longer serves us. Let me make the point, however, that denying our emotions is not an option—if they are genuinely felt and persist after we have questioned them. We must sit with how we feel—but hold off having any leading relationship conversations until we are back on an even keel.

One way of becoming present in the face of a "flimsy emotion" is simply to take a deep breath—or three. Often, shifting in your seat is enough to release the hold of an emotion. I also find that a mantra such as "They are doing the best they can from their perspective" helps me plumb the depths of empathy and compassion, which are needed to soften my reaction. I call these *leading relationship cycle breakers* because they can break the programmed "thought-feeling" cycle just long enough for me to gain a more objective perspective. Sometimes, the only way to break the cycle is to take some time out. Work out what is best for you and do it or ask for it—you may need to take time to work out what you need to do to move the situation forward.

The resilience factors can be an equally useful checklist in leading the relationship with yourself: you will no doubt have noticed how many of the skills and habits that you developed in part 1 are vital in successfully leading the relationship with others.

It Can Be Hard Work Sometimes, But Giving Up Is Not an Option

I have often found that in leading relationships, the darkest hour is just before the breakthrough is made. There have been times when I have worked hard to do all I can to alter the dynamic, and it feels like I'm getting nothing back. As a leader, I have toiled in my attempts to motivate, engage and support, and yet I'm getting the same old mediocrity. Then, just as I'm losing faith in the system, I notice signs that the magic is starting to happen. The shift has never failed to occur, either for me or for the many people I have coached. My coaching client, Isobel, described the "shift" in a letter to me:

> As you know, my new line manager didn't have all that much to do with me at first, and so her communication style wasn't a problem; but when my colleague was transferred to another team, that's when all the problems started. Over a period of a few weeks, I could see that she was beginning to talk to me in a condescending manner, and her overall attitude toward me seemed really bossy—and that made me feel nervous about the decisions that I was having to make in my day to day tasks. There was never any praise for the good work I was doing— only constant criticism. I put up with this for a while, as I told you, but as I was getting busier, I started to feel more and more inadequate. That was when I came to see you for some coaching. I was emotional when we met—it had been gnawing away at me for so long, I didn't realize until then how badly it had been affecting me. As a result of our sessions, I realized that I was allowing my manager to make me feel inadequate and unable to reach decisions. Our discussion about the reasons for the way she was behaving really helped me see what she might be struggling with. I began to feel positive feelings toward my

manager. The first meeting I had with her after our session was the best meeting I had ever had with her, and she even praised me! All these techniques have made me feel a lot more comfortable and confident in my role. I know now that I can change the dynamic in a relationship and take control over how I experience someone else's behavior. I feel so brilliant! I've had lots of meetings with her since, and it keeps working! It's made such a fantastic difference!

Another coaching client of mine describes her experience in a different way:

When I first started my sessions with you, I wasn't in a good place career-wise. On paper, everything was fine. I had a good job with a good salary in a market-leading company. I had been working there for around eight years and was generally well respected and considered to be an asset. In my head, however, I was a fraud, and it was only a matter of time before someone realized that. I felt as though that time was fast approaching, and my boss was onto me. I had come to the conclusion that the only solution was to find another job. Luckily for me, the HR director at my company realized something had gone wrong, and she encouraged me to think about getting a coach. I have to confess that I was dubious to begin with. I felt that my relationship with my boss was damaged beyond repair, that my work-life balance was completely out of kilter and that I was constantly underperforming both in the office and at home.

What I didn't realize when I started working with you was how important I am in my life. Everything that I thought was happening to me was filtered through my subconscious belief that I wasn't good enough or that I was about to be exposed.

I wasn't working with fact, I was working with the stories that my subconscious was telling me. My relationship with my boss had deteriorated, but I now see that *I thought* he was saying that I wasn't good enough. You taught me to listen to him with warmth and compassion. He may have been speaking to me in a dramatic or condescending way, but I began to realize that wasn't necessarily because he thought I wasn't performing, it was because he was stressed about meeting his targets and about the number of tasks on his to-do list. Realizing that let me respond to him in a way that wasn't defensive, and I found that, gradually, the way he spoke to me improved. He started to treat me as an ally. Or maybe he always had, and I just couldn't see it. All this was achieved without confrontation. The only change was how I interpreted his behavior. You told me that I could not control other people's behavior, but that I could bring it into my zone of influence. I didn't believe you at the time, but you were absolutely right.

A Final Word

I deeply care that my message has touched you—and inspired you to consciously lead in the relationship with yourself so that you are able to be the best of which you are capable, every day. This is my purpose and my passion. I have seen how these tools and techniques have changed people's lives. I wish I could coach you personally and travel with you on this journey, but I know that it's just not possible to work with everyone, and so I have tried to be with you through the medium of this book. My deepest desire is that this book can serve as your companion when you need advice and your cheerleader when you need support. Relationships are the source of our greatest joy, and when the hiccups arise, I hope you will return here, to remind yourself of what to do and how to be, to ease the relationship back onto a happy course. I wish you love and joy in the lifelong relationship with yourself, and much fulfillment in your relationships with others.

THE FIRST THIRTY DAYS OF LEADING IN A RELATIONSHIP WITH OTHERS

I want you to experience the transformational effects of leading a relationship with others by shifting your thinking and perspective about them, and so I've set out a couple of exercises that you can focus on in the next thirty days. I've chosen that period of time because it's long enough to enable you to ritualize these habits and to experience the significant difference that the new way of thinking will have.

The Devil's Advocate Exercise

It's time to wheel out your internal coach—the devil's advocate—again. He is going to test the quality of your current thinking and see if a more helpful or constructive way of thinking can be found so that you can shift the dynamic in a relationship that is not working well at the moment.

I'd like you to think about someone with whom you are not currently enjoying a good relationship dynamic. When you call that person to mind, what thoughts dominate about his or her behavior, intentions, motivation and view of you? How would you summarize your dominant thinking about that person? Assuming your dominant thought is negative, and you feel a negative emotional reaction when you think of him or her, we have found your "stuck thinking." Your DA is going to ask you a few questions about that stuck thinking.

1. What is the stuck thinking? (Write down the thought so that you can see it clearly.)
2. How is this thought hindering the relationship in this situation? (Set out clearly how this thought is holding the relationship back.)
3. How is this thought helping you or the relationship in this situation? (Set out clearly any assistance that thinking in this way is giving you or how it may be assisting the relationship.)
4. How much, on a scale of 1 to 10 (10 being the highest) do you want to change the way in which you are thinking about this situation? (Set out your score. If it is less than 5, write out why. This would normally only occur if it is helping more than it is hindering, in which case reflect on why you have labeled it as "stuck thinking." It may also be because you do not care sufficiently about the relationship to do the work required to shift the dynamic.)
5. What new thought or way of thinking about the other person would be more helpful? (Write down the thought or way of thinking that would be more helpful, using toward/positive language.)

6. When you see the thought written down, how does it make you feel and how closely do you identify with it? (This question is directed at whether you believe you can make the change and whether it will work. See How to Maintain Your Motivation, in chapter 3.)

7. If you feel negative about or unidentified with the new thought, can you select a different thought with which you do feel identified?

This section of questions completes the first step of the habit-forming process.

8. When might you feel the impulse to revert to the old way of thinking about the other person? (Write down the impulse points or environment where this is likely to occur.)

9. How can you plan to overcome the impulse to revert to the old way of thinking about the other person? (Write down the strategies to overcome the impulse.)

This section of questions completes the second step of the habit-forming process.

10. In what other ways does the stuck thinking have a negative influence—perhaps it has an impact on a wider group of people linked to you or the other person in the relationship. (Write down any other ways in which the stuck thinking may have an adverse impact—the more examples you can come up with, the better.)

11. What can you do to maximize the opportunities for repeatedly applying this new way of thinking to the relationship?

This section of questions completes the third step of the habit-forming process.

12. What would success look like if you approached the relationship on the basis that this new way of thinking was absolutely true? (Write down the ways in which the relationship might be affected by this new way of thinking.)

13. Are the positive consequences of making the change worth the effort? (This refers to step two in the How to Maintain Your Motivation section, in chapter 3.)

14. Is there any mental rehearsal or visualization technique that you could use to support your appetite to make the change and help with the development of the neural pathways? (In answering this question, it may help to look at the relationship room technique found in the appendix.)

15. What other support might help you habituate this new way of thinking? (This refers to step four in the motivation section in chapter 3. Please think about anyone who could act as a sounding board to help support you through the effort of attempting to lead this relationship.)

This section of questions completes the fourth step of the habit-forming process.

I recommend that you keep a note in a journal of the changes you notice over the thirty-day period after you have completed the DA exercise, because then you will be able to track the point at which the new thinking becomes less effortful, and the relationship dynamic begins to change.

The Warming Relationships Exercise

Relationships are all about making a connection. Strong connections occur where there is warmth, and warmth is developed in a relationship by setting an intention and focusing on building that connection.

Select a relationship where the level of warmth is less than you would like. Test your appetite to build the level of connection—if you feel internal resistance to the idea, explore your thinking about why that might be. Once you have a settled intention to build warmth in the relationship, then choose three of the following habits to develop in this relationship.

1. Expressing genuine appreciation of the individual's strengths.
2. Expressing genuine gratitude for the role the person plays in your life or work.
3. Being committed to actively listening to what is important to them.
4. Taking an interest in the individual's objectives and concerns.
5. Smiling, using open body language whenever you are in the same space as this person.
6. Doing something kind for this person whenever you can.

Once you have selected three habits to develop, think/do these things as regularly as is appropriate over the next thirty days. Use the relationship room technique set out in the appendix to build a warm connection too. Notice how the level of warmth develops and how the ease in the interaction improves.

APPENDIX

How Visualization Works

Our Brain Frequencies

When neurons fire together, they exchange charged elements that then produce electromagnetic fields, and these fields are what are measured during a brain scan. Humans have several measurable brain-wave frequencies, and the slower the brain-wave state, the deeper we go into the subconscious mind. The brain-wave states are:

- Delta (deep, restorative sleep, totally unconscious)
- Theta (a state between deep sleep and wakefulness)
- Alpha (the creative, imaginative state)
- Beta (conscious thought)
- Gamma (elevated state of consciousness)

Beta is our everyday waking state. When we are in beta, the thinking brain or neocortex is processing all the incoming sensory data and creating meaning between our external experience and our internal representations of that experience. Beta is not the best state for visualization or meditation because, when we are in beta, our outer experiences appear more real to us than our inner experiences.

Alpha is a relaxation state in which we start to pay attention to our inner experiences. When we are in alpha, we are in a light state of meditation or visualization—like daydreaming or using our imagination. We normally move back and forth between the beta and alpha states. If you've ever lain on a beach, with the sun warming your skin, and drifted gently off into a daydream, then that was the alpha state.

The theta state is when we are half awake and half asleep. This is the brain-wave state in which we are at our most "suggestible." In theta, we can access our subconscious mind because the analytical mind is not operating. Imagine you're lying on that beach again, and as the warm sun caresses your skin, you move more deeply into your relaxed state, drifting between wakefulness and half-sleep. That's the theta state.

Visualization Exercises for Leading the Relationship with Yourself

At step four of the habit-forming process, you are invited to use the resource of your subconscious mind to support the speedy ritualization of a new, more empowering thinking pattern. Following are some visualization processes that will be useful, together with explanations of how and why they work.

Overwriting Disempowering Thinking Patterns

Stage One of the Visualization Process

Find a comfortable place to sit where you won't be disturbed for ten minutes or so. Relax in the chair and notice your surroundings, without focusing on anything in particular. Now close your eyes and take five deep breaths, inhaling the air in through your nose and out through your mouth. (This is the opening sequence of the visualization process.) Think about the habitual-thinking pattern that you want to change and the feelings associated with it. Apply words to those feelings. See the words spelled out in front of you. The words are your description of how you feel; stressed, anxious, worthless—whatever they are—imagine that you can see them in solid form, made out of gelatin. Yes, gelatin. Give them whatever color you would like; stress may be made out of red jelly, anxiety out of yellow jelly and so on. Now, imagine a pirate's treasure chest and watch as the words float into the treasure chest. Once all the words are in there, imagine that you have a padlock and key in your hand. Move into the image and see your hand pull the metal arm of the treasure chest lid over the loop and fix the padlock in the loop so that the padlock is securing shut the treasure chest. Snap the padlock shut and hear that satisfying click that tells you it is locked. Look around you and notice that you are standing at the seashore. It's a beautiful summer day, and the sea is calm. You can smell the saltwater and the sand baking in the warmth of the sun. You can feel the light breeze against your skin. You feel strong and empowered, knowing that those old emotions have been discarded and locked away. You notice a boat nearby. You walk toward the boat and climb aboard. You signal to people on the boat that you'd like them to bring the treasure chest aboard too. When the chest is brought aboard, the captain of the boat announces its departure, and you sail off on the smooth, calm sea. When you are far away from land, you ask the crew members to throw the chest overboard. They are happy to help you. Before they throw it overboard, you take the key from your pocket and unlock and open the treasure chest, making sure the words are still inside. You watch as the treasure chest containing the words splashes into the sea, lid open, and then disappears slowly below the surface. You imagine the chest sinking all the way to the bottom of the sea and being lodged in the sand. You imagine the words floating out of the chest and dissolving in the water until they disappear entirely. You notice how free and unburdened you feel, liberated from the box and its contents. The boat returns to shore and you disembark, feeling light of step.

Take a moment to enjoy that feeling before slowly counting to ten and coming out of the visualization process. Open your eyes. Notice how you feel. (This is the finishing sequence of the visualization process.)

How Does This Work?

Let's look at some of the science behind why this visualization process works. Dr. Wilder Penfield of McGill University carried out hundreds of experiments in inducing artificial recall by applying a galvanic probe to the exposed brains of persons undergoing surgery for focal epilepsy.[20] The experiments produced convincing evidence that the past is recorded in time sequence and in detail in our memories. He found that the electrode probe evoked one single recollection rather than a mixture of memories or a generalization. He discovered the remembered record continued intact even after the subject's ability to recall it had disappeared. His experiments led to four conclusions of significance to the understanding of feelings.

1. The brain functions as a recorder of the events of our lives, the most deterministic of which occurred in early childhood. These recordings are in sequence and are continuous.
2. The feelings that were associated with past experiences are also recorded and are inextricably locked to those experiences.
3. We can be physically present with someone in the here and now, but our mind can be miles and years away.
4. These recorded experiences and the feelings associated with them are available for replay today in as vivid a form as when

they happened. Events in the present can replicate an old experience, and we not only remember how we felt, but we also feel the same way. We not only remember the past—but we also relive it; though much of what we relive, we don't consciously remember.

The objective of the stage one visualization exercise is to create distance between the feelings and the thoughts, and to alter your perspective about the link between the two. We do that by first imagining the words made of a flimsy substance (like jelly) and then by carrying them out to sea and watching them dissolve. This ability to create the imagined distance between ourselves and the feelings helps us to generate subconscious "space" to choose a different way of thinking and a new emotional response. When a pattern is triggered, we have an internal experience, which was represented by the words you locked in the treasure chest. This visualization process enables you to see the experience as external to you, which allows you to see that you have a choice available in terms of how to respond rather than automatically repeating the pattern. The process creates a sense of detachment from the feelings you might normally associate with the event.

Stage Two of the Visualization Process
Again, I will set out the visualization exercise and then explain why it works.

Find a comfortable place to sit where you won't be disturbed for ten minutes or so. Relax in the chair and notice your surroundings, without focusing on anything in particular. Now close your eyes and take five deep breaths, inhaling the air in through your nose and out through your mouth.

Think about the habitual-thinking pattern that you want to change and the positive pattern that you want to adopt. Hear, see or feel the phrase that represents the new thinking pattern. Imagine that you are in one of your favorite places—perhaps on a beach or in the country, or lying in a huge bathtub. Feel the feelings that you normally associate with being in this place, notice what you see, smell, hear and taste. Immerse yourself in the joy of being there. Now, while remaining in your favorite place, allow your new positive thought to come to the forefront of your mind, and focus on the positive emotions that come up as you play with the sound of the thought in your head and the look of the key words. Give the words that you see in your mind's eye some color, texture and a sound. Enjoy being with this thought, and identify it with the core of who you are. Take a moment to enjoy that feeling before slowly counting to ten and coming out of the visualization process. Open your eyes. Notice how you feel.

How Does It Work?
Having established a sense of detachment between your old thinking patterns and the feelings associated with them, stage two is about building a positive association with your consciously selected thinking pattern and the emotions that arise from it. That association is most easily established on the back of preexisting positive associative feelings—linked to your favorite place. You are seeking to manipulate your neuroplasticity so as to create an automated association between the thought pattern and the imagined emotions. It is intended that these visualization sequences will be carried out alongside stage three of the habit-forming process: constant conscious repetition of the selected thinking pattern.

Stage Three of the Visualization Process
Find a comfortable place to sit where you won't be disturbed for ten minutes or so. Relax in the chair and notice your surroundings, without focusing on anything in particular. Now close your eyes and take five

deep breaths, inhaling the air in through your nose and out through your mouth.

Call to mind the consciously chosen habitual-thinking pattern and conjure up the positive feelings that you have associated with it. Enjoy feeling those feelings for a moment. Imagine now that you are in a situation where the new habitual-thinking pattern will enable you to fulfill your own potential and get the best out of others. Notice where you are, who else is there, what you see, hear and smell—focusing at all times on the positive associated feelings. Play out a forthcoming interaction or challenge in this visualization, remaining anchored to the chosen thinking and emotions, and notice how your ability to deal effectively with the situation and get the best out of those around you is enabled by the new thinking and emotional state associated with it. Enjoy the successful outcome. Focus on it and on how pleased you are with your new approach for no less than fifteen seconds. Take a moment to enjoy that feeling before slowly counting to ten and coming out of the visualization process. Open your eyes. Notice again how you feel.

How Does It Work?
The final stage in the visualization process is to focus on how the new thinking pattern and feelings associated with it enable you to deal effectively with any upcoming challenge or interaction that you may be concerned about. That mental rehearsal process will generate increased confidence to deal with the challenge, and that, in turn, will have an impact on how you will behave, specifically in terms of your tone and body language, when engaged in the challenge or interaction. The more frequently this visualization exercise is carried out, the stronger the subconscious association will become, the more powerfully your tone and body language will support your message during the interaction, and the more you will feel calm and confident and easily able to deal with anything that arises.

I recommend that you record the visualization exercises, so that you can listen to them as you do the visualization activity.

Building Desire to Achieve Your Goal

We have spoken about setting goals that align with your purpose and are based on intrinsic motivators, and about developing habits that support the achievement of your goals. However, willpower is still initially required until the habitual thinking or action becomes ritualized. Developing an emotional charge for the fulfillment of your goals, and therefore for the development of habits, can help provide the additional motivation necessary when willpower is lacking.

Carry out the opening sequence of the visualization process. Imagine that you are sitting in front of a "visualization screen"—like a movie screen in a cinema. Call up an image that represents the achievement of your goal. Perhaps it's a work role you want to fulfill because it gives you the opportunity to contribute in a way that is meaningful for you. It may be the enjoyment of a relationship with a loving partner that you want to meet or delivering your message in a way that will make a difference to others. Engage all five senses in the image: What do you see, feel, hear, taste and smell? Enjoy exploring each of these five senses. To powerfully link the emotional connection with your image, you could stand up—keeping your eyes closed and your connection with the image—and raise your arms in a "victory stretch," adding a cry of achievement as you do so. The last section may sound a little strange but it does have the immediate effect of intensifying your emotional connection to your goal. Now, focus on how the current habit or habits that you are cultivating are going to bring you closer to the achievement of your goal. Perhaps the habit of thinking compassionate thoughts about yourself, so that you develop a loving relationship with yourself, will enable you to develop a healthy and loving relationship with another where you are not looking for them to "complete" you or make you feel that you are lovable. That will automatically make you more attractive to another. It may be that you are developing the habit of working smarter and focusing time and energy only on the things that will bring you closer to your purpose. You may be cultivating the habit of thinking thoughts of love and gratitude toward your romantic other so as to improve the relationship with the goal of creating a secure family environment. Perhaps you are developing the habit of committing one hour per day to focusing on an activity that will enable you to complete that business plan or write that book. Finally, it may be that you are devoting one hour per week to planning business development activities in order to develop your business in a particular direction. Taking action on a daily basis toward your goal and creating a strong emotional connection with your goal will hugely increase your chances of achieving it, especially if it is a goal that is intrinsically motivated.

When you have created a connection with the image of your completed goal, remember to use the finger and thumb trigger to develop an association with that feeling of anticipation, excitement or desire. Then end the visualization by using the finishing sequence.

Meeting Your Future Self

This visualization exercise is another way of connecting with your current goals. It's one of my favorite visualizations, though I find that it's sufficient to carry it out perhaps only three or four times a year, and so it feels like a bit of a treat when I do it.

There is no need to have a particular question in your mind as you go into this visualization, but simply to be open to the information that might come to you as you do it.

Carry out the opening sequence. Once you are relaxed, imagine that you are standing on a landscape. Look around the landscape and see what you notice, using your five senses. If you are on a beach, you may notice the sound of the waves, the smell of seaweed in your nostrils, the feeling of the wind in your hair and a subtle taste of salt on your tongue as you breathe in the fresh air and take in the scene before you. If you are standing in a meadow, you might feel the tickle of flowers on your legs as you walk through the long grass, smell the sweet scent of the honeysuckle and taste the warming morning air on your tongue as you take in the wonderful views. Create a picture that makes you feel relaxed and uplifted. Once you have settled on your landscape and enjoyed if for a while, begin walking toward something you notice off in the distance. At first, it appears as a tiny speck, but as you draw closer, you notice that it is a bench, and there is a person sitting on the bench. As you get even closer, you realize from the person's posture that this is your future self. Walk up to your future self and take a seat on the bench beside him or her. Look carefully at the face of your future self and assess approximately—or exactly—how many years older you are than the age that you are now. Your future self may only be a couple of years older—or twenty years older. Reflect on what you might usefully be able to learn from yourself about the progress toward your current goals or, more generally, the achievement of purpose in your life. Sit with your future self for a while and enjoy the warm feelings that pass between you. When you are ready, ask a general question such as "What is it you have to tell me?" or "What can I learn from you about the coming years?" Pay attention to any feelings, sounds or sights that you notice. Sometimes it takes awhile for your future self to "open up," so please be patient and just enjoy the experience. Pay attention to what comes up and ask any follow-up questions that occur to you. Notice how happy, fulfilled or desolate your future self appears. I have only ever had a positive aspect of myself appear, but some of my clients have had negative aspects of themselves emerge that has motivated them to make certain changes, like moving to a new job or exercising more. Sit with this visualization as long as you wish. Sometimes, it is comforting to meet a healthier future self, for example, and you might want to enjoy that sense of hope and positive expectation about becoming more healthy. Your future self may seem calm and fulfilled without any of the agitation that you currently feel, and that, too, can be a great comfort. You may also experience a positive reaction from your future self to a plan that you are formulating that firms up your resolve to pursue it.

Once you have reached the natural conclusion, end the visualization exercise using the finishing sequence.

Building Self-Admiration

I'd like to explain this visualization process using the experience of a client of mine. My client had an issue with "liking" herself. Her inner critic was overactive, with the result that she estimated that she spent several hours of her day thinking about things that had gone wrong in the past. She admitted that only a small part of that daily rumination was constructive, in the sense that she focused on specific things that she might do differently in the future. Following our first coaching session, it became clear that one of the key issues she had was that she was very hard on and unloving of herself. One way of building a more constructive outlook was to help her recognize her own strengths and attributes and build some self-affection.

She carried out the opening sequence of a standard visualization exercise. I asked her to imagine that she was in a landscape of her choice. She went through the process of filling in the details of her landscape by using each of her five senses. I asked her to envision that she was with her ideal self in the landscape and to focus on what the attributes were that made up her ideal self, to spend time noticing those qualities and how they had helped her ideal self achieve the life of her dreams. She concentrated for a while on the imagined life of her ideal self and how her dreams had been fulfilled. Then I directed her to ask her ideal self some questions. The first question was what the ideal self thought were the best qualities that my client had right now. When my client recounted the visualization to me later, she told me that her ideal self had been lying on the grass in the meadow she had imagined they were both in, she could see the lips of her ideal self moving, and she could tell from the loving look that her ideal self was recounting some positive aspects relating to my client, but she just couldn't hear what she was being told. The next question my client asked of her ideal self was what she needed to do to build the strengths and attributes to the level that her ideal self had achieved. The same thing happened—she couldn't hear what was being said.

After the visualization had ended, I asked my client what meaning she took from her inability to hear what she was being told by her ideal self. She immediately recognized that it was because she wasn't ready to believe it. As she repeated the visualization exercise, she began to hear more clearly what she was being told, and her confidence grew, together with a genuine self-liking.

Visualization Exercises for Leading the Relationship with Others

When you are committed to leading in your relationship with others, you will use all the resources available to you to do just that. Your subconscious mind is a valuable resource, and the following visualization techniques will be useful in your quest to be the leader of your relationships with others.

The Relationship Room

If you feel a level of antipathy toward someone, or a level of anxiety about what they think of you, then that will leak out in every interaction and take you down the relationship spiral. Shifting your fixed thinking is easier than you might think and is the most powerful means by which to begin to improve the relationship dynamic.

Find a comfortable place to sit where you won't be disturbed for ten minutes or so. Relax in the chair and notice your surroundings, without focusing on anything in particular. Now close your eyes and take five deep breaths inhaling the air in through your nose and out through your mouth.

Once you are comfortable and relaxed, spend some time creating your relationship room. This is a room that you will come to frequently in your imagination, and where you will convene with those whom you want to positively influence or build a powerful relationship with. It is a relaxed space that you find comfortable and which would be welcoming to those whom you invite to join you there. Think about the colors and textures of the walls and the furniture and imagine the layout of the room. Reflect, too, on how light or dark you would like the room to be. Play around with it—there's no budget, so you can decorate and furnish the room exactly as you would like it to be! It's important that you are able to build a positive association with this space in your imagination.

Once you are clear about how the relationship room looks and feels, you will be able to visit it in your imagination as often as you need to. Remember that the main purpose of the room is to spend time "interacting" with those whom you want to positively influence or build a relationship with.

What you will be doing in the relationship room is bypassing your habitual thinking blocks to get to your creative mind-set, which is difficult to access without quieting the mind.

After the opening sequence, enter your relationship room. Sit down and imagine that the person you want to interact with is entering the room. Do what needs to be done to make him or her feel welcome. Take a moment to enjoy sharing the space together. Feel or see the pleasure the person is expressing in spending this time with you. Engage with that image until you feel settled and positive about being together. Even if the odd negative thought arises, let it go and breathe deeply, tuning in once more to sharing the space with the other person. Once you are settled, ask the person what you want to know. For example: "What is important to you about our relationship?" "Tell me what you are afraid of." "What can I do to build our relationship?" "What can I do to show you how sorry I am?" "What are you interested in hearing about from me?" "Where has my thinking been faulty in our relationship?" As you ask the question in your mind, look at the other person, sit with the question between you until you "sense" a response. Because your subconscious mind is inductive, it will give you a response, but it may come as a feeling or a knowing or a sound. This works in the same way as going to sleep with a problem and waking up with a solution. If, before you fall asleep, you think of the problem and ask for a resolution, your subconscious mind will work on it as you sleep. Remember, the conscious mind switches off when you are sleeping. In the same way, in visualization—because you are in alpha or theta state—it becomes easier to access your subconscious mind and all the information it will have picked up that has slipped by your conscious mind.

Once you have the information you need, notice how connected you feel with the other person. Focus on that bond. Reinforce it by saying something that you might not tell him or her in person: something that makes you feel a little vulnerable perhaps, but will build an imagined feeling of warmth between you. Sit with that thought and notice what information comes up.

At the end of the interaction, thank the other person for coming and watch or feel him or her leave. Once the person has left, sit as long as you like in your relationship room, reflecting on what you might do with the information you've learned, and notice how you now feel in the context of the relationship or about the forthcoming meeting or phone call. Anchor that positive feeling by squeezing your forefinger and thumb together or squeezing your wrist. Then, counting from one to ten, come out of the visualization.

I, and those whom I have coached, have had some incredible insights while using the relationship room technique. For example, I've gained a realization that the other person, who seems aggressive and controlling, actually feels vulnerable and insecure. That appreciation will cause you to behave differently when you next meet or speak, and that will start to alter the relationship dynamic; you may become more compassionate yet assertive, rather than defensive and frustrated. Perhaps the visualization exercise will cause you to alight on an issue that is likely to come up that you hadn't really thought about and would like to do some more work on. Chances are, that before doing the visualization routine, you had a nagging feeling there was something more you should be doing, and the exercise has helped crystallize your thinking. In the case of one of my clients, he moved from fearing to respecting his boss—just from one visit to his relationship room. He "learned" about issues his boss had to deal with that he himself hadn't focused on before, and he understood why that was making her behave in the way that she was. He respected her being able to do her job so well despite those things. It really doesn't matter if you think you are "making it up" while in the relationship room; what matters is whether what you've "experienced" has changed your thinking or feeling, or both, because that will change your behavior, and in turn, the relationship dynamic will begin to alter.

Switching Your Focus with Gratitude

Sometimes relationships which generally work well, can go through a bumpy stage where niggles and irritations arise. If you find yourself in such a situation, then this technique will work to remedy your irritation and to get the relationship back on track.

Go through the opening sequence and into your relationship room. Call the other person in the relationship into the room. Greet him or her warmly. The principal purpose for calling the person into the room is to relate all the things about him or her and what he or she brings to your life/work that you are grateful for. After you have welcomed the person, begin relating what was the first great thing that you noticed about him or her when you met, and how that attribute has served to strengthen your feelings of warmth toward the person. Relate the ways in which he or she has enhanced your life/work and recount specific occasions when you have felt enriched in that way. Tell the person what you would most miss if he or she were to disappear from your life. By this stage, feelings of warmth and genuine affection should have arisen in you. This is the point at which to ask what the person needs you to do or be, in order to get the relationship back on track. Notice that you are not asking what you have done to make things go awry but rather what you need to do for things to work well. Sit quietly as words or feelings come up in answer to your question. Just like before, you subconsciously know what needs to be done, but your conscious mind will have been blocking the answer. The solution may be to have a candid conversation about the issue, or to express gratitude for something that has been done or simply to come from a place of warmth and affection in your next interactions with the individual. Follow the exit sequence from the visualization. Keep at the forefront of your mind the aspects that you most appreciate about this person and make a solid plan for getting the relationship back on track.

ABOUT THE AUTHOR

Emma. J. Bell was a top-ranked employment lawyer who spent almost twenty years litigating over broken relationships at work. Emma has been designing and delivering leadership development programs for the last fifteen years to enable leaders to fulfill their personal potential and to motivate and engage team members. She has been acting as facilitator and coach to boards and partnerships whose relationships have broken down at the senior level.

Emma lives in Scotland with her husband, Graeme, and their Jack Russell, Buddy. Visit Emma online at www.emmajbell.com or www.emmajbell.co.uk.

ACKNOWLEDGMENTS

I owe a huge debt of gratitude to many people for bringing this book into being. Firstly, to all the people in the corporate world and in the public sector whom I have been lucky enough to work with—those who have shared openly in our coaching relationship, those who have trusted me enough to be vulnerable so as to enable their business to flourish or those whom I have accompanied on a journey through a leadership development program. You have taught me as much as I ever shared with you.

To my editor Mark Chait: I loved your "no-nonsense" Brooklyn style. Without you, this book would look very different. Thank you.

To my fabulous advisory panel: you were the first people to honestly appraise the material in this book, and your feedback gave me tremendous comfort and courage, and your tips were incredibly useful. Thank you.

To my cheerleaders—you know who you are. You helped me find my voice so that I could share my message. I love you.

NOTES

Chapter 1

1   Matthew A. Killingsworth and Daniel Gilbert, "A Wandering Mind Is an Unhappy Mind," *Science*, vol. 330, no. 6006 (2010): 932

2   Ibid.

3   Ibid.

4   Christine Comaford, "Got Inner Peace? 5 Ways to Get It Now," *Forbes*, April 4, 2012.

5   Sharon Begley, "Your Child's Brain" *Newsweek*, February 18, 1996, 55–56.

Chapter Two

6   Shai Danziger, Jonathan Levav and Liora Avnaim-Pessoa, "Extraneous Factors in Judicial Decisions, *PNAS* vol. 108, no. 17 (2011): 6889–6892

7   Alvaro Pascual-Leone, Amir Amedi, Felipe Fregni and Lotfi B. Merabet, "The Plastic Human Brain Cortex," *Annu. Rev. Neurosci.* 28 (2005): 377–401

8   I. Dar-Nimrod and S. J. Heine, "Exposure to Scientific Theories Affects Women's Math Performance," *Science* vol. 314, no. 5798 (2006): 435

9   Phillippa Lally, Cornelia H. M. van Jaarsveld, Henry W. W. Potts and Jane Wardle, "How Are Habits Formed: Modelling Habit Formation in the Real World," *European Journal of Social Psychology*, vol. 40, no. 6 (2010): 998–1009

Chapter 4

10   Rush University Medical Center, "Greater Purpose in Life May Protect Against Harmful Changes in the Brain Associated with Alzheimer's Disease," *Science Daily*, May 7, 2012, http://www.sciencedaily.com/releases/2012/05/120507164326.htm.

Chapter 5

11   *Stanford Prison Experiment* http://www.prisonexp.org

12   Albert Mehrabian, *Silent Messages: Implicit Communication of Emotions and Attitudes*, (Belmont, CA: Wadsworth, 1980)

Chapter 6

13   Amy Harris and Thomas Harris, *Staying OK,* (San Francisco, CA: Harper & Row, 1988).

14   K. H. Rollings et al., "Empathic Accuracy and Inaccuracy. In S. Strack, ed. *Handbook for Interpersonal Psychology: Theory, Research, Assessment, and Therapeutic Interventions*, (Hoboken NJ: John Wiley and Sons, 2011), 143–56

Chapter 7

15 Matthew McKay, Martha Davis and Patrick Fanning, *Messages: The Communication Skills Book*, (Oakland, CA: New Harbinger, 2009), 32.

Chapter 8

16 Alix Spiegel, "Teachers' Expectations Can Influence How Students Perform," NPR, http://www.npr.org/sections/health-shots/2012/09/18/161159263/teachers-expectations-can-influence-how-students-perform

17 K. H. Rollings K.H. et al., 143–56.

18 Michael Morris; Janice Nadler; Terri Kurtzberg; Leigh Thompson, "Schmooze or Lose: Social Friction and Lubrication in E-mail Negotiations," *Group Dynamics: Theory, Research, and Practice*, vol. 6 no. 1, (2002): 89–100

19 Sara Lazar, "Meditation Experience Is Associated with Increased Cortical Thickness," *Neuroreport* vol. 16, no. 17 (2005): 1893–1897

Appendix

20 Wilder Penfield with discussion by L. S. Cubie et al., "Memory Mechanisms," *AMA Archives of Neurology and Psychiatry 1952*, vol. 67: 178–198.

Lightning Source UK Ltd.
Milton Keynes UK
UKOW04f2030161215

264829UK00003B/38/P